Choices: Your Life is What You Make It   *Kelly McGiffin*

CHOICES:

Your Life is What You Make It

by
Kelly McGiffin

Choices: Your Life is What You Make It   Kelly McGiffin

Choices: Your Life is What You Make It   Kelly McGiffin

This book has been a journey of reflection and, as I was writing it, I couldn't help but immerse myself in the memories of my upbringing and my life choices since. Now as I reflect on the body and messages within the piece, I want to dedicate the book to my Mom and Dad. As you read through this body of work, you may get the sense that my father (in particular) influenced me negatively on many occasions, and while there were some hard lessons through him, I realized long ago that these two people simply did the best they could in raising their family.

    The context of any story is critical in really understanding its messages. My parents married very young (20 & 17) and suddenly were responsible for a full family, long before they were ready or were prepared for. The pressures of raising children while figuring out their own lives at such an early age, escalates that pressure immensely and the decisions you make along the way are simply destined to be flawed; and they were.

    The entire point of this book is that many people in our world are handicapped in this way, as they are raised. Some much more so than in my case, some lesser but what you do – yourself –

as you make your own choices, becomes your responsibility. When faced with a difficult situation, people have two choices; do something about it, or do nothing about it. The easier course on the short term, is do nothing; find an excuse, blame your environment, deny the ability to act.

As are we all, my Dad and my Mom were flawed individuals and their decisions and the outcomes of those decisions had a bearing on my (and my siblings') environment, however, they were never intended outcomes. They made decisions both considered and impulsive, based on what they thought was needed at the time; and they created certain situations and ultimately lessons that I tried to build on.

My parents have passed now and I miss them in many ways, they divorced in my late teens and my mom and I stayed close and I miss her greatly. My dad and I were not real close near his end but we also were not estranged. We had found an adult relationship that was comfortable, if not close. I was able to see both of them shortly before they passed and said my heartfelt goodbye.

I hope that their role in this book of lessons and choices help to illustrate the everyday decisions that people make can and will have broader outcomes than you likely realize; and more importantly, that no matter what those influences are, you alone determine your best life.

Choices: Your Life is What You Make It   *Kelly McGiffin*

Choices: Your Life is What You Make It   *Kelly McGiffin*

"Excellence is never an accident. It is always the result of high intention, sincere effort, and intelligent execution; it represents the wise choice of many alternatives - choice, not chance, determines your destiny."

— **Aristotle**

Section 1: **Introduction**

Your life is yours alone, and it is what you determine it to be.

Your life is defined by the choices you make; it is forged and shaped by every decision of whether to act or to not act. Regardless of your circumstances, *you* determine what you are willing to do, what you will not do, what you really don't have the appetite to do, and even what you believe you have no choice but to do.

Every child is born into the world with complete innocence. At birth, everyone is pure of heart, without ego, without insecurities, and with no bias. As we grow, those around us will teach, guide, influence, and sometimes manipulate us either directly or indirectly, and this molds us all into the adults we eventually become. It is a flawed process that people have questioned, blamed, praised, and misread for an individual's success or failure as participants in our world.

Are we defined by these influencers and the environment we are born into, or do we have an innate ability to rise above these pressures and determine our own destiny? This question is the basis of the age-old argument about nature versus nurture.

In this book, I don't attempt to definitively answer that question or even raise the debate, but I do have one important message—it is the same message that I've tried to send to my children and my grandchildren, with admittedly mixed results:

Your life is what *you* make it. It is about your choices, your approach, and your response to the events that take place around you, as well as your response to incidents that will invariably happen to you— your lessons.

As a child, blame can be placed on your circumstances, your environment, your influences, your tragedy, your parent's shortcomings, your lack of resources… the list is infinite. However, as you become a thinking, choosing and mature individual you, and only you, choose your path and each step you take along that path.

My message to my children has been simplified in this way:

"I wish only two things for you as you grow up— be happy and be responsible. If you accomplish that, you will have a great life."

I've followed that with the explanation that they will have trouble finding one without the other, for they are codependent.

If you're not responsible you will find it hard to be happy; too much left undone will start to affect you sooner or later. There will be no peace for you to enjoy happiness.

And as for the other side of that token, you'll never sustain responsible activity if you can't find a way to enjoy your life around that quest. It will become unbearable drudgery.

Having driven that message and attempted to foster that foundation, here's the follow up advice, and the ultimate guide to accomplishing both objectives—

If you don't like your life, change it.

"It's not that easy!" many have said, including my own children, upon hearing this. It's especially difficult in the throes of a bad job, or a bad relationship, or a failure at work, etc. And they're right, it is hard…but its not impossible either.

It appears for most that when one wants that change to happen immediately (let's say tomorrow) through a giant leap, it becomes daunting and viewed as a mission impossible. One simply cannot shortcut the many processes that are worthwhile. You cannot get there (to the change you want) from wishing it to happen, only from working at it and making it so.

No matter the challenge in life, minor or major, the change mechanism is never what I call a 'light switch' moment. There is no 'easy button' outside of television commercials.

So, my counter is this: When you focus on the steps you need to ensure that this change will come, each step will get you closer. The change you want is down the road, rarely next door, so start walking toward it. Change in your life *is* easier than people understand, care to admit, or are prepared to pay the price for.

If you want out of a bad relationship, you can get out but it will take some big decisions, likely some pain, and certainly some insistence that it *will* happen. You have to decide that it's going to happen, and that you will not backslide or compromise. When you get to that point, it becomes a conscious choice, and you will find a way through the discomfort.

Often people compromise their stated wish to transform because they haven't fully come to the decision to make that change. They sabotage their choices by inventing roadblocks largely based on an inside desire to stay where they are. There is something about the current situation that they don't want to give up, whether it's a small comfort piece, a hope that things will improve, or something that holds them back from really making the choice they say they want to make. In each instance, other factors are blamed.

If you are in a bad job, you can decide to make a change. You can apply for other employment, you can augment your education to make you more marketable, or you can look outside your current community for a wider array of opportunities. You can either move forward, or you can stay and attempt to make your current job better. There are choices you can make in every scenario to change your employment situation.

What's easiest is throwing up excuses and using them to then give up on the process.

"I'm stuck. I have no choice!"

Rarely is this really true, and, in most cases, it's simply weakness. It is a clear decision in its own right. Your choices—your life.

Choices: Your Life is What You Make It   *Kelly McGiffin*

Lesson: *Time to Grow Up*

Choices: Your Life is What You Make It   *Kelly McGiffin*

Choices: Your Life is What You Make It   *Kelly McGiffin*

Growing up I had a little brother (Kirk) two years younger and a sister (Kerry) five years younger until I was about 14 and my other sister (Jo-Ann) came along. My dad always let me know that I was the oldest and my job was to protect the other kids. He made no bones about the job of a man, even a little man.

    My grade one started in September and I didn't turn 6 until December and as I look back, I was ready intellectually but not emotionally. I loved school, got me out of the house and those older brother responsibilities, even then. The problem was that I was a shy boy and enjoyed the cocoon of my own world, so even though school had its wonderful attraction for me it also created its own terrors – socializing. It was unpleasant at times but it was compartmentalized for me and the good outweighed the bad as I could always stick to myself and put the invisible walls up.

    I knew my role, even at 5, and was able to get my time alone in my own head, in between helping with the 'kids' and averting my dad. My dad was an affectionate guy but he drank on weekends and we either got the gushing lovey drunk, or the don't go around him angry drunk. When he was drinking, I'd just as soon stay clear of either if I could. He was a violent man in a starkly black and white world. Never violent with his kids and never physically with my mother. However, he did have his outbursts and was a scary man at times.

We were living in a small town; Port Alberni, British Columbia. A forest industry-based town that was booming economically back in the early sixties and looked just about the way you would picture it. A quaint small town with wartime houses all over, a main street with both a Woodwards, and a Woolworth store centering the 50's style street presentation. The shops were clean and streets were safe.

At this time, we were renting a small house just down the street from my Uncle Lloyd's house, a few blocks from Auntie Peg and another block from my Granny's home. I'd walk to school, about 8-10 blocks, with my older (by a few months) cousin Billy, and I was feeling pretty grown up for a five-year-old.

I remember being very excited about Christmas that year, even though we were what I'd call 'very poor', and I didn't ever get much. I had been especially good and wanted, so badly, a garage set with some small cars and I just knew Santa was going to bring them this year.

One day early in the school year but close to Christmas, I was walking home from school with Billy and our neighbor-kid Lonnie, and was telling them about my excitement for Christmas and how I was sure Santa was going to bring me that garage and cars this year. They laughed and told me I was just a little kid and that Santa wasn't even real. They said it was all my parents and if they didn't have the money, I wasn't going to get it.

I was so angry that I was going to fight them right then and there. Now I was pretty scrappy, so Billy was afraid of me, but Lonnie was older still (a year, maybe two) and I was pretty sure that he could whoop me, so I just kept my anger inside, and decided I'd just tell on them to my dad instead. Discretion is of course, always the better part of valour.

When dad got home and we were all having dinner, I told him what those older boys had said to me and I knew he was going to validate my anger. How could those boys slander Santa, especially at this time of year? My dad said nothing, he just kept eating and looking down at this food. My brother at 4, and my sister (not even a year old) were kind of oblivious to the whole conversation. I thought it was weird that he said nothing but, in our house, you just didn't push things because you never knew what the trigger might be to bigger things.

When I got up the next morning, my dad brought me into the bathroom with him and sat me on the counter by the sink, he began shaving (which like all little boys I loved to watch) and then he stopped, looked at me and said:

"You know what Billy and the other boy said about Santa? Well it's true son, there is no Santa. It's just mom and I that give you presents each year."

I heard little more than that second sentence…

"It's true son, there is no Santa."

At 5 years old, it was like my childhood ended. My heart literally sank into my chest, and I honestly felt like someone had just murdered a member of my family. Dramatic? Perhaps, but these were the real emotions and sentiments of five-year-old me at that moment, a moment I've never forgotten.

My dad clearly saw the tears well up in my eyes and start streaming down my cheeks. And as rough as he was, he stopped shaving, put his arms around me and seemed to try to make it better.

"Now that you're grown up and know these things, you can help us on Christmas Eve and you get to fill the stockings for your brother and sister." he explained, using his best Tom Sawyer exuberance to sell the shift in focus.

Like somehow this was going to replace the loss I felt? I was almost angry with him for the suggestion. It felt like he had not just murdered Santa but was now minimizing just how important this person had been to me. I feigned appreciation and promised to keep the secret, and to get excited about truly becoming Santa's helper, but the lump in my throat and pit in my stomach were not as easily fooled as my father.

One of the things I learned that day, was that innocence is a fragile gift that is easily broken and can never be replaced. A lot of kids figure out the Santa project, but it's usually much later and goes unsaid in most homes. It's treated with a grin and a wink to preserve the childhood and its comfortable fantasies and reassurances that young kids seem to need to fully develop without unnecessary fears or stresses of the real world.

I went to school that day, feeling all the fool, injured and yet the painfully matured. As silly as this may sound, at 5 years old, my childhood changed that day. It began the hardening process, and nothing seemed to surprise me from that point on, although many things should have. It was the start of many pains, none enough to kill, only enough to chisel, perhaps scar but certainly enough to shape a life.

And yet, in life's bigger picture, it also forged me into a person that refused to look back and feel sorry for myself. I accepted the role as Santa's helper and vowed not to have my brother, sister, and eventually my own kids ever have to go through that feeling of the rug being pulled out from under them.

Christmas magic has become sacred to me over the years, and I relish the wonder and excitement of kids at that time of year. I've never told any of my kids about Santa and when they asked, I always reply "Well I believe in Santa" because I do.

My life has been all about moving forward and making choices that will move me forward, never allowing myself to wallow in the pity pool. You can extend the mourning over the bad things that happen to you, or you can realize there's nothing you can do about what happened, only about what you'll do next. Learn and move forward, make sure that even the most difficult lessons make you better.

I tell people, even as a CEO, where your reaction to bad news can have repercussions far along down the line. Give me a day or two to understand the context of the bad news and I will begin the planning of how we move next. That will become my focus, not of what just happened. Oh, I'll take the time to understand what just happened, to make sure I (we) learn from it fully, but the primary focus for action will not be wringing of hands or the blame process, it will be where do we now need to go.

They say whatever doesn't kill you makes you stronger… Maybe. I'm not totally sure about that, but I do know that my own failures have certainly made me smarter or at least wiser. They wouldn't have, had I failed to recognize my own culpability. If I blamed everyone and everything else rather than take responsibility and try to better understand what went wrong, I would have likely made the same mistakes.

Life's lessons are somehow cosmically designed to be that – lessons. But lessons are useless if you refuse to learn them.

Lessons and Choices: *Lessons and Choices both Brought Me Here*

Choices: Your Life is What You Make It   *Kelly McGiffin*

Choices: Your Life is What You Make It   Kelly McGiffin

To this point in my life, I've had some successes and have carved out a pretty comprehensive resume. I'm 64 and recently retired as a President & CEO of a large Canadian Credit Union, and as a baseball/softball coach I've participated and led teams at the Provincial, National and International levels.

My background and upbringing may surprise you as we go through this journey, but I pride myself on starting with virtually nothing and achieving some modest National and International prominence in my field(s).

I do not have an MBA, nor did I achieve any other University or College degree before starting out in business. I have never played professional sports, nor was I ever considered a major Canadian prospect in my youth in any sport. I have never written professionally, nor have I taken public speaking or writing accreditations. Yet I became a prominent and successful Canadian business leader, a Nationally and Internationally acclaimed coach, a popular speaker/presenter on leadership, and have written several published articles on banking, leadership and now this book.

How does one achieve that without the normal qualifications? Work, muster the courage to do something new, learn from mistakes, try again, research, prepare, and constantly move yourself forward. Choices, each and every one.

Section 2: **The CEO**

Choices: Your Life is What You Make It   *Kelly McGiffin*

Choices: Your Life is What You Make It   Kelly McGiffin

I worked for 42 years in the Canadian Credit Union system moving my way up from the font line to the CEO chair. My last tenure at FirstOntario Credit Union started with my entry in November 2007 as President & CEO, and I took this organization from $1.3 billion in assets under administration to over $5.2 billion when I retired in January 2019 (11 years).

During that time we increased membership from 60,000 to over 120,000, increased retained earning by $78 million (the company had only achieved a total of $38 million in the previous 68 years), increased branches from 17 to 32, and we introduced several leading community contributions which included a decorated volunteer program, a vast student nutrition project, international co-op funding, student housing, and an affordable housing project.

While FirstOntario has risen into one of the most visible, successful, and influential financial institutions in Ontario over this last decade, the humble beginnings and challenges faced in our first few years have become distant memories.

This story in itself is worth telling. When I arrived in 2007, it was on the heels of a long (8 months) strike that included violence on the picket lines, arrests, and ultimately had been settled through binding arbitration.

If you are not familiar with this mediation process, let me just explain that while it achieved a back-to-work solution, it was not a solution to the ill feelings and morale of this organization. Management was still entrenched in their positions on the issues, and employees were bitter about the experience and lack of progress. The result was a new CEO, and I was the lucky candidate.

We rolled out a plan of what *could be*, rather than what *had been*. I held a full company-wide meeting in a large conference hall, and I went through my observations and plans. I asked the entire group of employees and management to create a new organization built on going after business, rather than cutting costs.

The previous management had looked at their P&L and analysis of their key performance indicators (KPI's) and determined that their only course was to tighten the belt and get costs in line to improve those numbers. The two key focuses were staffing costs as a percentage of assets, and their efficiency ratio (cost as a relation to income – or how much does it cost to generate a dollar). Both were extremely high for the industry, and the logic was to cut those significantly – to right the ship.

The problem was that management realized that within the current organization many jobs were unionized and therefore any move to reduce staffing costs would be met with resistance. So, as a gesture of good faith, they first reduced such things as management vacation, management benefits, management staff perks, overall celebrations, branch upgrades, etc.

This strategy ultimately backfired when union staff were not alright with carrying on in the same manner come contract negotiation. I came to the organization a few months after settlement and needed to refresh this company.

I looked at this a little differently. From my analysis, after experiencing 31 years in the BC credit union system where there was strong acceptance for credit unions as a banking alternative, Ontario was well positioned to learn about, and be convinced of the same value of alternative banking. I felt that this was particularly true of the FirstOntario branch footprint where the demographics of a working-class potential was more evident than in the core GTA.

I believed that the correction of KPI's was likely better achieved through gaining business, and therefore gaining income rather than cutting costs. Now cutting costs is a holy grail for many; the old saying goes – it's not your money, so control those costs carefully. I can't disagree with that sentiment, but I believe that money sitting is money not invested. And I firmly believed that an investment into this market was both warranted and necessary.

There is another old saying in business: that you can't shrink yourself into greatness; and another equal and parallel saying in sports: that if you are only on defense, you are playing 'not to lose', which can ultimately and invariably be a good team's downfall.

I find many organizations so focused on playing 'not to lose', that they rarely find ways to win. FirstOntario had fallen into that trap, because, after all, it is a much easier and safer route in business to play that way. It is not a strong long-term play, but one that attracts many leaders coming into a new environment. One thing that is very evident in business: Culture is only a biproduct of your leadership and, as a result, it can transform in a heartbeat – to the negative. Choose the wrong leader, or a leader that takes the organization to a different track, and your culture will change— much more quickly than you might think. If that happens to be a negative trend, it is a mighty hill to slide down, and even mightier to climb back up.

It's not as easy to get back to a positive culture. You have many more disbelievers and 'play it safe' individuals than creative, courageous leaders in most organizations. It's a condition that is quite normal in society. It involves two ingrained mindsets: be skeptical of other's new ideas to insulate yourself should those ideas go bad; and: don't take the risk if you can't guarantee the win— the table stakes are your career.

These natural pessimisms can be much more easily nurtured into a negative culture than a positive culture. Further, its not difficult to demotivate people, as negative actions are often felt immediately, while positive actions are held in a 'yeah but' state for a period of time, as the receiver looks for proof that the positive actions are for real. In other words, it's very easy to disillusion happy people but very difficult to make disillusioned people happy.

Now then, the key question for me entering this new organization became, *how do we unlock the potential of this organization to go after that huge market right in front of* us? As I like to keep things simple, I broke the strategy down to a logical sequence. First thing's first, we needed to do an analysis and present it in a form that helped to create the idea, and ultimately convince the team, that we have a compelling opportunity.

I called a company-wide presentation after a few months on the job to ensure I understood the landscape both internally and externally, while studying those opportunities. I started the presentation by simply outlining the facts as I saw them.

In the West, Canadian credit unions had population penetrations of close to 40% (members to population); in Ontario that ratio was around 10% and indeed much lower in our FirstOntario communities. And yet we sat in biggest market in Canada— Ontario!

This alone was compelling, if we really believed in what we offered— I'll get to that in a moment. Our ability to convince Ontarians (particularly those in our footprint) should be achievable, as clearly there was such resonance in other areas of Canada.

Even more compelling was the average assets held by members in other credit unions. Peer comparisons from across the country are extremely helpful in forming a valuable context. The average assets held within their credit union per member literally measured how much business on average that a credit union could expect from fully engaged members.

Measuring these two simple ratios gave me some idea of context and more importantly, theoretical opportunity.

Here were some of the facts when I arrived at the end of 2007 (facts in public annual reports compiled at the time):

Members at FirstOntario – 67,000
Assets at FirstOntario (on balance sheet only) - $930 million

Assets per Member:
FirstOntario	Ontario CU's	BC CU's
$13,880.00	$17,132.00	$27,010.00

Members to Populations:
FirstOntario	Ontario CU's	BC CU's
5.82%	10.23%	38.63%

Simple extrapolations:

    FCU Assets could be at the levels below, should we be able to move our members to use us at even our peer's levels of Assets per Member (more business from current members)

At the Ontario Rate	At the BC Rate
$1.15 billion	$1.8 billion

    The number of members FCU could increase to, should we convince members to join us at our peer levels of population penetration

At the Ontario Rate	At the BC Rate
114,000	456,000

    Now I realized that 40% penetration of the population was likely not achievable in our trade area; however Vancity, a credit union carved out of a similar urban demographic was able to penetrate to 14.83%, proving a metropolitan CU in a large center could achieve higher than the current 10% in Ontario. So, at 14.83%, member levels could conceivably reach 177,000 members. It was therefore not inconceivable to suggest that FirstOntario could grow to a range of $1.8 billion to over $3 billion if we could grow membership and bring in more business per member, on average.

    It had been done elsewhere, why not here?

Painting a positive and yet realistic picture of where we could go was not difficult, and it was clearly predicated on a proven business study of what other credit unions had actually achieved. I'm certain that the logic had my audience thinking, "OK, that makes some sense." But it was equally, and certainly much more exciting to hear the new leader suggest it was both achievable and going to be one of our objectives.

Now they could go from down in the ditch, reeling from a bitter strike, to a company that had a pretty bright future with real, contextual market opportunities; and they had a new leader prepared to take them toward them.

The next and bigger part of the plan was to make the adjustments internally that assured the culture shifted toward the new opportunities. In my estimation this would require both a demonstrated change in internal investment, and a self-imposed discipline to walk the talk of those values at every turn— for an extended period of time.

I warned the Board that this process would make things worse before they got better, but that the overall investment would pay off. This would not ordinarily be an easy sell, but the Board, like every other scarred stakeholder, was beaten to the point of thankfully embracing new possibilities. They almost felt like they had nothing left to lose. Lucky for me, their change in paradigm was at the right time, the right place, and was the right read on the environment.

We opened the purse strings and started to refresh the feeling in the organization. We reconstituted the Christmas party, expanded expense accounts, made coffee free in the branches once again, changed out their furniture, initiated a branch-refresh program to update all branches, and look at new branch opportunities. Then we spent on marketing and we pushed new products offering very competitive features.

We rolled out an aggressive plan to go after business, and to reward growth and entrepreneurial approaches. I dismantled the project teams where I found they held meetings to discuss projects and whether they were red, yellow or green lights for what seemed hours, if not days. They (the project meetings) were the epitome of the old saying 'death by committee', as the group took great lengths to debate why a project should be yellow rather than green, and how that might affect the project and its outcomes per the charts attached.

While I wanted things to be tried and tested before perfected, we needed to get them out there and make them happen. I was prepared to have a few failures, and I did not condone recklessness, but rather a short test period to have a reasonable confidence that they worked, and then get those offers out there.

If we had to use manual systems because the technology wasn't perfected, so be it. Get the service or product out there for the member (customer) and make their experience great. They didn't know (or shouldn't know) if it was onerous on the administration side. We would start that way, and streamline later.

Now having explained the theory of *'deliver and not wait for perfection'*, there were really not many deliveries rushed out ahead of working effectively. The timing and delays of the old project mentality had been bogs and were no longer getting in the way, so it worked.

We decentralized lending authorities to give discretion back to frontline managers and business development people. This was actually a major move for our change mechanism. The trend in the industry was to cut down approval time and staffing error by adjudicating credit based on scoring systems. Most FI's had moved to this system, and I believe it was more designed to keep staff costs down rather than customer experience improved; however, I felt that if we were basing our differentiation on relationships, how could we allow a simple matrix to determine lending decisions?

We rolled out this aggressive and invested plan in the spring of 2008… and the Lehman Bros. fell in August.

I remember calling my team together and saying to them, "Well, we have two choices: pull back and start laying off (as our neighbors had already begun to do), or we control costs where we can without compromising this plan, and go for the growth while everyone else is pulling back."

We did the latter and, perhaps not surprisingly, we took off and never looked back. In the next several years, from December 2007 to my retirement at the end of 2018, the organization grew to $5.2 billion in assets under management, grew to more than 120,000 members, and branches grew from 17 to 32. We put a new state-of-the-art banking system in, we contributed millions to our communities in terms of student nutrition, affordable housing projects, naming rights of key community facilities, international cooperative development; we offered some of the best rates ever offered to our members, introduced completely free checking accounts, AND we produced more than $78 million net earnings back into our reserves.

In context, this organization, through penny pinching and caution, had turned in only $38 million to reserves in the previous 68 years combined. FirstOntario became one of the most successful turn arounds in Canadian credit union history.

Choices: Your Life is What You Make It   Kelly McGiffin

Section 3: **The Coach**

Choices: Your Life is What You Make It   *Kelly McGiffin*

Choices: Your Life is What You Make It   Kelly McGiffin

Ever since I was a young boy I've loved baseball. I mean, I *love* baseball. I'm not sure if it was the appeal of the history, the smells, sounds and colours involved (which are so vibrant and awakening for me), or just the fact that it was the opposite sport that my dad excelled in. He was a hockey player, and a very good one from what I learned.

    I could spend some time exploring why I love the sport, but I don't really care and I doubt you do either. Whatever the deeper reason, baseball captured me, and I've been in its spell for as long as I can remember.

    I remember my first book, the Babe Ruth story. It was an amazing story of a boy that had a very rough upbringing who was forgotten by his parents for the most part, but who found his way in life through his immense baseball talent, ultimately becoming one of the most iconic sports figures in North American history. It was like a real life fairy tale—Cinderella of the sports arenas.

Choices: Your Life is What You Make It   Kelly McGiffin

    I saw my first World Series on television in 1968 with the St. Louis Cardinals playing the Detroit Tigers in a best-of-seven final. I was 12 years old, turning 13 in a few months, and I had not seen very many colour televisions in my life to that point. Suddenly, I was watching this vividly coloured celebration of American sport play out in front of me each day, as the boys and male teachers (that was the way it was in those days) huddled around the new television in the science room at school.

    I remember the Cardinals' bright white uniforms with scarlet trim, and the iconic bird on bat symbol across their chests all being in stark contrast to the monotone black-and-white Tigers uniforms. The games were played in those beautiful green carpeted cathedrals with red, white and blue banners draped everywhere.

    At that age, I knew little about the game, other than playing some sandlot type pickup games, but it didn't matter. There were plenty of subject matter experts in the room. The World Series of 1968 catapulted my interest into hyper speed, and I soon became a most passionate fan.

    I followed the Cardinals (who lost the series), and for a while I multi-tasked in following the Dodgers on the West Coast. It was my love of the Dodgers history that really appealed to me. Roy Campanella, Duke Snider, Maury Wills, Sandy Koufax and those legendary Dodger uniforms with that Dodger blue. Then Canada got their own team, the Montreal Expos, in 1969. That was all I needed.

    I collected baseball cards, baseball magazines, newspaper articles, anything I could get my hands on. In the late 60's and 70's there was no internet or access to news other than the traditional mediums of newspaper, magazines, television, and radio. So, I had minimal access, and a very slim budget to get other than old publications or free ones, so my collections were, and are, small and precious to me.

Nevertheless, the sport consumed me, and I started to play the game at every opportunity. I grew up with three very supportive and close relatives. My brother, Kirk, and my two cousins, Tony Powell and Rob Shick. Some of you that are hockey fans might have heard of Rob, as he went on to have a long and successful career as a referee in the NHL.

Kirk, Tony, and Rob are all two years younger than me, but we were all small growing up and so it wasn't like I towered over any of them. We were so close that we really grew up like siblings, and to this day we continue to act more like four brothers rather than cousins.

When it came to baseball, our larger family had a very full history. As I understand it, both Tony's father (Aubrey) and Rob's father (Earl), my uncles, had been scouted and tried out for professional teams in their youth. Aubrey was a catcher, and Earl a shortstop.

The apples didn't fall from the tree with those two, as Tony went on to a US College career and played on Canada's National Team; and Rob, while focusing more on hockey, was an All-Canadian in men's fastpitch softball—a common alternative to baseball in Canada. And Kirk (our dad was an exceptional hockey player having played at the semi-pro level) may have had as much talent as either of those two, but was smaller and less interested than any of us...especially when he discovered girls.

That left me, and there is no doubt that I was the worst of the four, hands down. Ironically, I loved baseball much more passionately than any of the group, and yet I was clearly the least talented.

Anyone that has had a younger sibling that turns out to be much better than them at sport, or school, or games, or anything, will understand the insecurity and frustration it can cause. Try multiplying that by three— all at once.

There was no jealousy on my part, there was no maliciousness festering, and there was never any teasing or embarrassment from any of my brothers. In fact, they were always very supportive, flattering, and helpful wherever possible. They also defended me through any critiques that might come from others, although few did.

The environment, however, fuelled me to look for every edge possible to try to even the playing field. I not only wanted to be good at the sport I loved, but I wanted to stand shoulder-to-shoulder with my peers, my family. I sought out information at every possible turn, and the first real mentor I had in the world was Tony's father, my Uncle Aub.

I was a catcher growing up in minor ball, and my dad had made me a catcher to 'escalate' my game. He was a hard knocks guy, and Kirk and I often laugh about my first catching lesson with him.

My dad was coaching our house team, and Kirk and Tony both pitched. Rob was on another team, so he didn't practice with us that season. I was older, but because I was not very good the league allowed me to play down with the younger guys since my dad was coaching and he couldn't afford to run into town on two separate nights of the week for two boys. Small towns, especially back then, were quite accommodating.

He decided that if he caught me, my game, my catching the ball period, and my eye at the plate would get much better, much quicker, and I was, of course, game to do so. As I started the practice, he believed (rightfully so) that one of the first orders of business was to teach me how to block the ball on errant throws.

I teach this same drill today (as do many coaches) to catchers, and those that master it become priceless to pitchers, as they create a valuable trust as someone that will literally lay their body down to protect the pitchers mistake from causing damage to the team. When I put boys and girls through this drill however, I use whiffle balls, tennis balls, or some sort of softer ball than real baseballs. But you guessed it, my dad did not.

First off, and in fairness, he didn't have the resources to have different textured balls, so real baseballs were all we had. He threw them in the dirt, ball after ball, and my job was to flop down in front of them to block them…and I did.

I became quite adept and fearless in the art, and I credit him for toughening me in this skill. The next thing he noticed however was that as a new catcher, I would flinch, especially when a batter swung— both a flawed habit and a dangerous one, as the catcher exposes the unguarded side of his head and neck.

My dad would remind me each time, but I couldn't break the habit. Finally, he said to Kirk,

"You pitch and I'll stand in, and swing through the ball to make sure he (me) gets good habits." He walked Kirk out to the mound and was talking to him for a few seconds, and I thought he was likely giving him an idea of what the drill would look like.

Kirk had the ball, and just stood on the mound looking at me. We had no signals. He could only throw a modest fastball, and I wondered what he was waiting for. Just about then, my dad swung the bat backward and hit me square in the facemask. I was rocked straight back onto my butt.

I looked at Kirk, and his eyes were wide and his mouth was open in shock. My eyes were also wide open and I looked up at my dad, not knowing where to cry or yell at him. He looked down and asked,

"Are you ok?"

Other than the shock, I was fine and answered, "Yeah."

He said,

"There you go, you can't get hurt with that mask on if you keep your face forward."

In today's terms, it was an unimaginable lesson but it was the late 60's and so it was just a lesson. And incredibly, all those hard knocks lessons worked, and I made my first all-star team the next season (in my own age group) as catcher.

Uncle Aub watched me struggle that first year, and while my dad had been able to give me the basics behind the plate and the opportunity to play there, Uncle Aub saw I could do more and that I wanted to learn more. He'd talk ball with me at every opportunity, watch the games on tv with me, and was my own colour man for the games we watched. He had a great sense for the game, and a great appetite to teach it. Tony didn't really need the lessons, he was the real deal as a player and everything he touched in baseball was at another level.

Like most gifted players, Tony never could coach, even later on. He just couldn't describe how he hit, or pitched, or fielded. It was just natural to him. Sure, he learned some skill additions as he played at higher levels and could pass those along, but he rarely scuffled in sports, and so he had a hard time relating to those that did. Many very talented players have a similar difficulty in relaying this in the coaching world, and it is very likely why you don't see the best of players doing much coaching.

That is certainly a generalization, and I've been around great players that can add great value to other players in terms of teaching, but you often find that the guys that scuffle in a sport, scrambling to learn, investigate, and try every possible edge they hear about, become some of the best coaches.

Not only can they depart the trial and error process effectively, often having spent countless hours thinking about mechanical sequences and studying both positive and negative outcomes of such adjustments, but they study the game to an obsessive degree looking for those edges. Their minds are open to constant learning, looking for THE ANSWER.

Perhaps the greatest side benefit of the 'scuffler' is that he or she knows both the feeling and frustration of failure in the temporary and longer term; and also, the invigoration of finding that ANSWER, at least short term.

I was definitely in the scuffler category, and Uncle Aub made a difference for me. He opened the window of baseball subtleties that I grew to truly appreciate; the way a pitcher and catcher set up a hitter several pitches ahead of the 'out' pitch; that every pitch in a sequence should have a specific purpose and when it doesn't, it's usually just a lazy thinking process; that offensive and defensive strategy can be enhanced by pre-thinking the opposition and/or be done on the fly by what you learn in any given scenario; that batting orders matter, from a two-way psychological perspective; that where certain hitters bat in the lineup can affect the psyche of their own players *and* affect the psyche of the other team.

The result was that I grew into a player that worked very hard at the game, and transformed myself into a solid player. I really came into my own as a player once I left my home town. Once I was out from under the shadow of my rather talented family, I came to realize, through results and other's comments, that I was always one of the top players in whatever *other* community I lived in.

It could have been, and is actually quite likely, that all my hard work was simply paying off at that time, but now I also attribute my playing success to me being better than I had thought. When you constantly compare yourself to siblings that are more talented (and as it turns out, exceptionally talented), *and* they are younger than you, it can't help but affect your confidence; and confidence is a major component in sport.

The point of this reflection on my playing ability and my passion to learn the sport, is that it all culminated in preparing me to coach as I entered my thirties. Even in my twenties, as a vocal leader (even if not the playing leader), I was thrust into a captaincy or player/coach. The basic rule of thumb in senior sports is that if you open your mouth, others are more than willing to let you lead, or in their terms, let you do the work.

Section 4: **The Communicator**

Choices: Your Life is What You Make It   *Kelly McGiffin*

Choices: Your Life is What You Make It   *Kelly McGiffin*

Choices: Your Life is What You Make It   *Kelly McGiffin*

Lesson: *Strengths Are Built Through Trials*

Choices: Your Life is What You Make It   *Kelly McGiffin*

Choices: Your Life is What You Make It   Kelly McGiffin

I had plenty of lessons from my youth. In fact, not long after the Santa discovery we moved out to a very rural location, a good 10 miles from town, which, in those days, may as well have been 100 miles. On our little gravel road, we had our few neighbors and immeasurable untapped forest, as green and magnificent as you can imagine. Moss covered logs, fern groves, tall fir and cedar trees everywhere, clear watered creeks, and majestic natural clearings below the canopy of the endless coniferous giants.

We'd bought our place from one of those scarce neighbors, Art Tapley. It was a small ½ acre piece carved out of his own 40+ acres, and the house had been moved and placed on blocks for our arrival. There was electricity hooked up but that was it, and that is how it stayed for most of our ten years there.

Tapley (as we called him) owned a 40-acre ex-pig farm... ominous sounding now (due to the Picton horror of the 90's), but pretty cool back in 1962.

Choices: Your Life is What You Make It   *Kelly McGiffin*

He had been rumored to have been a lawyer at one time that had given up the corporate world to become a farmer. He lost the love of his life, let the farm run down, and was now a commercial fisherman that mostly lived on his boat, and more often than not, inside a bottle.

He was hardly ever at his place next door, which looked like a 1940's house owned by a hoarder; and when he was there, had no interest on what went on outside the one room of his house in which he lived. He had boarded up the rest of the house, almost as a statement of how he compartmentalized his life, and he lived in one room of squalor and left the rest of the house behind.

The older neighbor boys were already tired of country life, and regularly left the road to go closer to more gathering spots for teens and pre-teens, or they would take off to fish the streams in the area. Either way, they were rarely around, and when they were, they rarely had time for us youngsters.

As a result, for five or six years, Kirk and I had the run of at least the 40 acres that surrounded our little ½ acre, and it included not only acres of forest, creeks, and wildlife (some of the most beautiful you could imagine in the rainforests of British Columbia), but also the remnants of the old pig farm.

This included five separate pig pens, which were small wooden houses all with walls and roofs and doors, surrounded by their own fences. They kind of looked like little Hobbit huts. It also included a huge old barn complete with a cement floor, hay loft, stalls, and remnants of old tackle and saddles, etc., and a chicken coop with racks and hutches including the large chicken wire windows. This area also included a large open expanse on concrete that had a roof over it, and we found out later that it was the space for pig slaughter; and it included a hoist, large fire pit, and a boiling barrel or pot for heating up and shaving the pig's skin after the killing, before final butcher.

This entire section of the farm had also acted as Tapley's dumping ground of past decades, and had old cars and trucks from the 20's and 30's, etc., and had old machine parts, junk, you name it. For the next several years, it became our own personal playground.

Our property, cut out of a section of Tapley's on the road, was surrounded by his property, and as such there were no barriers as to his or ours; and without his presence, it was just viewed as ours, at least by Kirk and myself. Other than the old farmstead, there was forest everywhere, including a creek that ran about 50 feet from our house, trailing and winding down for acres from the mountain above us.

Good thing the creek was so close too, because without running water, one of my early chores was to take a pail down to the creek every morning and every afternoon, and fill a giant plastic garbage can in our kitchen with the water we needed for that day and the evening... water for drinking, washing, cooking, etc.

So, before describing my play time, let me tell you a little about my chore time. As the oldest, I was charged with water duty every day, and after dinner with emptying the slop pail. This means we had a metal pail under our sink that caught the water that my mom used to wash the dinner dishes. She'd heat the water in a kettle on the oil stove (our only heat in the house), and wash the dishes. When done, she'd empty the sink's water by unplugging the sink and letting the water drain into the pail.

Every night I had to haul the slop out and empty the heavy pail. Food washed off the plates and floated at the top. It was the grossest job ever, I thought... until later; and because we basically ate what my mother called goulash (which was ground beef, spices, and elbow noodles mixed in a white sauce of some kind— I hated it), and a lot of Mac n' cheese, elbow macaroni was forever floating on the top of this greasy, gross water when I hauled it outside for dumping. I still can't eat Kraft Dinner to this day.

The other thing we ate was puffed wheat, sometimes for breakfast, lunch, and dinner. Not bad with a little sugar on it. It seemed that at every month's end, just before any income came, whether it be pay or social assistance, puffed wheat was all we had the last few days. It's an existence, not a fond existence, but I tell you what, I never had much of a weight problem.

My chores, for the most part, were filling up the house water every day and watching the kids. My parents liked to party... every weekend. And every weekend from the time I was about 8, I would watch the kids while they went out. Terrifying times, I'll tell you. Ten miles out of town, no plumbing, doors that didn't lock, power that would go out regularly, heat from only one room, and a television (black and white) with one channel that went off at midnight. I would sit in the kitchen (the only room we'd open in some winters) with a butcher knife, a candle and matches, and a flashlight (if we had one with good batteries) for what seemed like every Friday and Saturday night until 2-3 in the morning, waiting for my parents to come home from the party or dance they'd gone to.

I was literally terrified every time I had to watch the other kids, but had little choice. I had to watch my little brother and sister. It was my job as the oldest, and yet all the while, I had no idea what was on the other side of the door at any given time. There was a lot of wildlife in our area, cougars and bears, and so a kid's imagination can run wild.

With no TV, no books, no-one else awake (the littler ones just fell asleep, trusting big brother to look after things), I turned to my baseball cards as my only entertainment, night after night.

Choices: Your Life is What You Make It   Kelly McGiffin

Now, I loved baseball. My dad was a hockey player and often tried to get me interested in that sport, but I felt it was quite violent (which you'll find ironic later), and for some reason, I turned to baseball. Like I admitted earlier, maybe it was the first full book I ever read – The Babe Ruth Story, or the fact that two my uncles (on my mother's side) had been prospects in the late 40's, early 50's with the Cubs and Yankees, or maybe it was just the vision of sunny days and green grass as the backdrop; but whatever the psychological cause, it resonated with me for as long as I can remember.

I especially loved collecting baseball cards. They were inexpensive, and I often fuelled my ability to get them by finding change in the couch or chair left by my dad after a drinking night. I'd secretly, diligently, save the nickels and pennies to buy the cards at every opportunity, and every once in a while, we'd get a bit more money to entertain ourselves (in the car) while dad was in the 'pub' having a few beers (which was often several hours).

Taking those cards out after Kirk and Kerry fell asleep (even though I pleaded with Kirk to stay awake— he just couldn't), I'd memorized the stats, the faces, the teams, the teams that they'd played for in the past, the positions they had played in their careers, and the highlights listed. I'd organize them into dream teams; build houses with them; categorize them by Nationality, by league, by color of uniform; anything to occupy my time. My choices were to throw myself into that, or just sit and let my imagination run... the worst thing I could allow to happen in my heightened state of fear.

I hated being in this position and as I got older, all I could think of was how could I get out of this family.

"When I grow up, I'm going do whatever I have to get out. I don't want to be the 'one' anymore, I don't want to be the oldest, and I just want to be responsible for me."

Choices: Your Life is What You Make It   Kelly McGiffin

    I was determined to make choices that would take me to a better life. I had no idea what that would look like, but I felt it had to do with school and study— things I was good at and that I enjoyed.

    Now, on to the play time. It was really a world of make-believe for Kirk and myself. My sister was five years younger, couldn't really keep up, and was not too interested in our activities. Kirk was only a year and a half younger than me, and we were best friends… well, we really were our only friends.

    We would run wild through the forest, building forts, using fallen trees for natural fortresses, finding clearings that looked like God had reached down and carved out a resting place for himself. We lived in a paradise of natural playground.

    Part of the appeal of the dilapidated farm surrounding us, was its fuel for our imagination. For us, this place that had the pig pens was transformed into individual holding cell units for the imagined enemy (usually the German army of the 2nd World War, in my generation— remember that war had just ended about 20 years prior to this time frame), and the barn and chicken coop became prisons we had to either infiltrate or escape from.

    Further down the creek, just past the barn that ended the farm portion of Tapley's property, was 'The Dam'. It was clearly an old dam he'd made decades before that had fallen down in most parts and water flowed over the top. But it still held enough water back to create a small fresh water pond. Just upstream of the dam was an area we called "Hell's River", a part of the creek that was overrun with skunk cabbage and devil's club which is a real plant made of a vine-stock full of barbs, like a cactus with green leaves, very prickly and very ominous looking. This section of the creek was dark, and the overhanging trees full of moss made this a place neither of us ever wanted to enter alone.

Near the dam were all kinds of old mechanical pieces. We never knew what they were really from, but in our world they were from a pirate ship that had sailed up the creek from the ocean when the creek had been a raging river (we did live on the west coast of Vancouver Island). According to us, it had sailed up that river to hide its stolen treasures, thus setting up many summers searching for the hidden loot.

Clearly, we could get lost in our imaginations summer after summer, day after day, in the majesty of this BC rainforest, and so my dad invented a good way to ensure his own self-comfort with our playing wherever we wanted. He pulled out an old referee whistle one day (he was a long-time hockey player, and I always believed he had beaten a ref to death to get that whistle) and he said,

"Boys, here's how it's going to work. When you hear this whistle blow, you better come running and you better be yelling your lungs out as you run letting me know you're coming. If you don't and I think that I have to put my boots on to come find you, and then find out it was simply because you just didn't answer... I will whoop the tar out of you."

Now, first of all: my dad didn't bluff, and secondly: he was known to all, including my own witness, as a very tough guy that could fight, and would fight any man for almost any reason. I wasn't sure if I had any tar in me, but I sure as hell wasn't going to find out, and when that whistle blew, we dropped everything where we stood and started running at full speed, yelling all the way,

"We're coming Dad, we're coming!!!"

Now I will take a short commercial break here to say: my dad never laid a hand on either of us in anger. He was a man not opposed to violence when it came to other men, but I, never in my life, witnessed or heard of him raising his hand to a woman, child, or even a lesser capable man. He hated bullies, and stressed the importance of defending anyone less capable of defending themselves, especially women; and I don't believe he ever could have raised his hand toward us kids. Nevertheless, he was a scary man, and we were not about to take that chance.

That whistle worked well for him, he never had to get his boots on, but it sure as hell was hard on us, especially when we'd get back totally out of breath and run into the house and he'd say,
"Oh there you are, I was just checking.... get back to what you were doing."

I mean, *really*?

I will admit that without toys (most of our guns for fighting the enemy were made of wood, sticks, or junk we found at Tapley's), we were actually pretty damn happy. Kirk and I found ways to play constantly. Not to say we were without toys completely. We had a few things like little green army men, some dinky toys we used in the dirt, and a few toy guns and holsters—every kid had those things in the 60's. So, we made use of what we had, but most of our toys were imagined or made from what we found.

I yearned for such things like toys, and in my future, I would ensure my own kids and grandkids never wanted for anything of this kind. This was not a great choice, as it proved to be an enabling practice that actually took away from them learning that you need to 'earn' the things you really wanted in order to truly enjoy them.

Those times of hard work, adversity, and what many might view as a tough childhood in today's terms, were clearly sprinkled with times of delight. The lessons I learned from both the experience and the retrospect of those times are about trumping your current conditions with the imagination of what *could be*, rather than just wallowing in what *is* at the moment. This has turned into a very valuable perspective.

I viewed this environment, this lesson, as the background for a set of choices that I needed to make, and that I continue to make in every situation; choices that guide me to find a better lot than I currently have. I do very little wringing of hands in tough situations. I look at where I want to go, plot out a course of actions, and begin to move forward toward that better lot.

You simply need to work hard at your responsibilities of the day, whether you like them or not. Avoiding them, or resolving that they are all you'll ever have, is not the same as working hard to accomplish them while using those very responsibilities to motivate yourself to be more, do more, and get more out of life.

The other main lesson for me through these early times was the use of my imagination, to dream of a different environment, a new way of life, a life that wasn't mine— yet.

The lesson: ensure that you use your imagination, it is not just a childhood tool. Use it to fuel the determination to improve your situation and to better plot your life's next steps— methodically moving step by step without compromising your current responsibilities because you're not satisfied today. Use your imagination to envision, believe and ultimately to know that you're going to build a new future.

Choices: Your Life is What You Make It   *Kelly McGiffin*

Section 5: **More Choices and Lessons**

Choices: Your Life is What You Make It   Kelly McGiffin

Choice: *Don't take your role lightly*

Choices: Your Life is What You Make It   *Kelly McGiffin*

Choices: Your Life is What You Make It   *Kelly McGiffin*

People will often talk about a leader's vision. Some never think they have it, and I wonder if that is because they've never allowed their imagination to run wild. When you can lose yourself in imagined worlds, it can be turned into a skill-development foundation that will allow you to imagine new scenarios and new end states. Take what you have now, or what is directly in front of you, and stop to imagine what you could do with that to move the environment forward and make it something more engaging and productive.

      Doing all those messy chores as a kid was not my idea of fun, and I was determined to find a better way in life. I think they stood well to teach me what I *didn't* want, and I often go back to my imagination days to help me envision what could be possible.

Choices: Your Life is What You Make It   *Kelly McGiffin*

Choice: *What Can Be from What is There?*

Choices: Your Life is What You Make It   *Kelly McGiffin*

Choices: Your Life is What You Make It   Kelly McGiffin

Time continues to tick no matter how successful you are at any one point in your life; the clock and calendar just don't discriminate. As I headed ever closer to retirement with FirstOntario, I worked toward a follow up of the cultural strategy that was designed to turn around the organization.

    I determined it was time for a new strategy that was only now advanceable based on that original scale play; and ever more urgent as we saw margins (basically the difference between what we pay for deposits, and what we lend those out to customers) in this financial institutional world dramatically compressing—forcing new focuses.

    As we faced the reality that, while currently successful as margins continued to decline, we were staring at some very significant challenges. Simple profit and loss (P&L) projections based on a declining income seemed to be a stark reminder that new imagination skills were needed.

As I thought this through, a new strategy developed and was forwarded to the Board and my executive team. It was two-fold: the margin business was failing and our organization and, in my opinion, every credit union, and indeed smaller financial institutions in North America, needed to establish a new financial model. I determined that we needed to dramatically attack the concepts of new income sources. This had been talked about in credit union land for some time, but no one had really tackled it to any extreme. I felt it was time.

In parallel, customer experiences were changing rapidly with exponential technological accesses, and offers for banking and payment services from outside the traditional FI world. We needed to reflect and rebuild our relevance in this new world. So, we set out to define and rebuild a new bar of customer experience (CX).

Let's go over the financial model discussion first. It's a classic business study that, as obvious as it may seem, is not and may not even be grasped by (many in) the industry until it's too late.

Like Kodak refusing to recognize and embrace digital technology, or Blockbuster ignoring similar social changes in preference and ease, credit unions in North America have just not stopped to study their competitors— the banks.

They have certainly paid attention to FinTech's, and there is an almost paranoid urgency to invent, align and/or combat those disintermediation's that are predicted to compromise their relationships with their members. I will cover that immense subject in the section under CX to follow.

The parallel and equal challenge, and the reason for this two-fold strategy, is that coinciding (and likely as part of the technological advances in banking, payments, and social media education) margins have declined dramatically over the last few decades.

Banking and 'credit unioning' used to be a pretty easy business. When I started in the mid-seventies, margins were double-digit. It's pretty easy to make a profit and use those profits to generate capital and profit choices. When I took over at FirstOntario 11 years ago, margins had already declined to about 3%.

When I left a few months ago, credit unions were averaging just over 2.16% and had declined from 2.58% since 2010. The banks were operating at about 1.61% and have operated that rate (1.51-1.72) for the last several years. *AND* the banks cost of funds is significantly cheaper.

So, here's the question I asked: if our main competitors are the banks, and their cost of funds are lower than ours, what makes us believe that our margin won't eventually have to drop again to the 1.5% range? And the follow up question is: what will that make our P&L look like if, and more likely, when that happens?

I decided to look closer at our competitors, the banks, to see how they were able to operate at such low margins. Their profit motive is much more vociferous than that of credit unions, so why would they be alright operating with a lower overall margin?

Rushing to a solution is what many managers in business love to do, they pride themselves on being problem solvers. There is no rush like being able to say and ultimately prove that you solved the problem.

The difficulty is that many times we jump to a conclusion before all facts, or as many facts as possible, are explored before a good thoughtful review can be done. Even at that, some statistical confirmations, evidences that can confirm your assumptions, etc. are always most advisable.

These are two quotes that I truly believe in:

"In the absence of information, we often jump to the most convenient conclusion. If we're wrong, we spend a lot more time and money than we needed to."

And:

"It's more important to seek to understand than to seek to be right."

I'm not sure of the origins, and they may be derivatives of the originals, but they are well worth noting.

As I looked at the banks, our major competitor *and* models of extreme commercial success, I noticed that they generated about half of their total income from margins and the other half from other income sources. This was enlightening to me, and so I looked at the annual reports for some of Canada's larger credit unions. It was amazing to me that the average split was about 90% margin source, and 10% other income. In the best cases I saw an 80/20 split and in the worst 95/5.

Without going into the differing abilities to generate new business income sources, which is as much a regulatory debate as an industry debate, here is the key set of questions that needed to be rhetorically asked of credit unions:

1. If the majority of your income sources are dropping dramatically and you have no other way of generating capital, what will you do?

2. If you believe your margins will not drop further, how can you compete with the banks and other FI's that clearly can offer better pricing?
3. If this was a business you were financing and it showed a decreasing income source and more likely drops to come, would you entertain financing for them or investing in them?
4. If margins are going to continue to decrease, have you done any P&L projections?
5. How much further can you cut expenses to combat this trend? And what will those cuts jeopardize or compromise?
6. Will you be able to grow your book or develop new business of any kind without a new capital source, which ultimately takes profit to generate?

Clearly, if this was any other business and 80-90% of their income was dropping like a rock and there were further drops to come, you'd be steering well clear.

I decided that the answer might be found in doing some more extensive research into how other credit unions had succeeded. In almost every instance of success, it had come at the good fortune of higher margin or merger windfall, and that success was either short-termed or declining (margin). Often the times coming are not seen until they're there.

So, I decided to look at "similar" but not exact industry comparisons; that of the banks and the Canadian pension plan models. In the case of the banks, I confirmed in general terms through their CBA (Canadian Banking Association) that indeed their reported net financial income (margin) was around 50% of their total income. In reviewing some of the Canadian bank annual reports, it was confirmed that those estimates were quite accurate. And I found that if we, as credit unions (often compared to banks in our business models), needed to get to a reduced reliance on margin, it certainly seemed that it had to be by developing new income sources, just as the banks had.

    Now the banks will tell you that credit unions have an even playing field with them. Many politicians will agree, mostly because the banks have a powerful and effective lobby; and for the most part it is a positive lobby for Canada. When it comes to an even playing field, that is not the case.

    Credit unions, until very recently— and only the very few that have gone to Federal regulation— are extremely limited in investing in any entity outside of their home Province. They are very restricted in owning subsidiaries, and discouraged and/or run askew of the Regulators should they even invest in property that may offer returns. As we know, banks own banks in the US, banks and properties around the World, trade in bonds, etc.

    Without a significant change in our Regulatory environment, and the subsequent sophistication to build a global presence, the bank model was not going to fit completely for answers. So, I decided to look at other models.

    I studied the World Bank Report, "The Evolution of the Canadian Pension Model" and discovered that in the mid-80's that Canadian Pension Investment leaders had determined that the returns on their traditional investment sources (largely government bonds and such other domestic traditional investments) were not going to match the expected needs of the pension funds going forward.

    They developed a new risk appetite and sought the appropriate expertise to develop new investment decisions. This has, of course, seen a huge success curve, and the Canadian Pension plans today boast one of the most successful and sophisticated investment portfolios in the world.

Could credit unions at least learn from this model? Were there alternate investments to consider beyond just taking collective deposits and lending those out? Were there safe investments that could render a greater return than a mortgage (which was at the time 3-4% return)?

These questions seemed answerable, and I created a new division within our organization through this strategy that was singularly focused on a new mandate. Find new, safe, and diverse investment forms that maximized return and created capital.

In the first few years, we generated millions of dollars in returns and, in given periods, they outpaced that of the margin side. The credit union, as I entered retirement, was clearly on the right track for changing its financial model. And as I reviewed their latest published reports, it's evident that this Investment Division at FirstOntario is carrying the bulk of income returns for them to this day, providing millions of dollars in return for their members; a legacy that I am extremely proud of.

There were, as a matter of course, challenges with this strategy, such as regulatory anxiety (new territory does that), Board continued courage (which wanes with the aforementioned anxiety), expertise accumulation (a non-negotiable), and overall due diligence costs to ensure strong and stable decisions.

The most prevalent of those challenges was the ever-changing Board appetite. Most credit unions face this challenge at their best of times.

Choices: Your Life is What You Make It   *Kelly McGiffin*

Choices: Your Life is What You Make It   Kelly McGiffin

Lesson: *A Word on Boards*

Choices: Your Life is What You Make It   *Kelly McGiffin*

Choices: Your Life is What You Make It   Kelly McGiffin

The democratic nature of credit union Boards, while well intended, can and in many cases are proving to be very damaging to progressive thought that must be more and more aggressive.

The Board environment within a credit union simply does not ensure or perpetuate the appropriate skill-sets and experiences to govern effectively. Most are filled by every day members that (frankly) have no business sitting on a governance board asked to oversee sophisticated financial decisions.

To put this in real context, lets explore the learning and skill-set path of an average credit union Board member. They are 'elected' by the membership from within the membership, and their backgrounds are rarely in Financial Institutions. After all, credit union members are reticent to support ex-bankers for fear that they are solely out to "destroy" cooperative values. The result is that credit unions get well intended members that have zero background in running a financial institution. They're intelligent people (mostly), and they're there with the right intention, however they do not know the business at all. What is their practical training to get that expertise? Let's explore.

Most will have 3-4 hours pre-reading for each Board meeting to help understand the business needed by the Board to review at that next meeting. Most Boards meet once a quarter, some once a month. And invariably they do extra committee work between Board meetings. So, lets use the time commitment for the most extreme case: a monthly Board meeting (four hours), with 4 hours pre-read; two committee meetings (two hours) in between, with 2 hours of pre-read. That amounts to 14 hours per month of preparation and discussion on credit union operations at the highest and most committed level, which would be considered an extreme example. That's 728 hours per year, if you believe this is done, 52 weeks a year.

This means from zero background in running a financial institution, as a Board member, you are now essentially learning the business in terms of becoming one of its most trusted advisors at a speed of 91 work days a year (based on 8 hour days).

Your CEO has likely worked in the industry for close to 20 years at this point, at a variety of positions, which equates to 5,200 work days (even at just 8 hours). The CEO has been appointed as the Executive entrusted to *RUN THE COMPANY*, and that reflects his/her experience, and the decision by the Board that he/she has the right leadership qualities.

Mathematically, it would take a Board member 57 years to gain the same specific and intimate understanding as the CEO. *(And remember, the number of hours is likely really half of the Board example above.)* This means most Board members will simply never be a true peer of your CEO when it comes to the business of running a credit union. You owe them (the CEO) the respect of that experience, not the doubt that many Governance experts suggest.

No CEO wants a rubber stamping Board (well, no good CEOs) because they need a group that can be sounding boards, test-and-learn partners, and ultimately stated and strong supporters of the challenges that the business faces. But no CEO deserves a Board, or a Board member, that thinks they can run the business better than they do; and that happens all the time.

The role on a credit union Board is to question and compare, to insist on proof, and to ensure correlation between plans, implementation, and outcome line up reasonably. It is not now, nor should it ever be, to operate or talk about how to better operate a business that they have no background in.

I have had several Board members decry the statement that they should not be discussing operational issues, other than in a strategic context. They rail at the idea that this should be off limits. This is ego, not logic and certainly not leadership.

One Board member said to me,
"Listen Kelly, if I want to know how much you paid for this pencil, as a Board member, I have right to find that out!"
My response:
"I have no problem with answering the question of how much that pencil costs. My question back, however, is why would you need to know that in your role as a Board member? What strategic value does it contain?"

The point here is that CEOs, and other Executives should never be afraid of answering questions or providing complete transparency, it is actually critical to do so… but the quest for that need to know by a Board member can go too far, and actually create a totally unproductive role for that Board member as well as others. Your questions need to have context and appropriateness, or they are a waste of everyone's time; and some can create a path that cycles you down a rabbit hole from which some credit unions never surface.

Many a credit union Board member has related a story of their own personal, or a 'relatives', experience at a branch, and that story has started a Board discussion on how that must be a problem across the entire spectrum of the organization. I am not exaggerating this leap in logic. It happens all the time, and it constantly has management defending <u>one</u> member experience… all this at a strategic Board table. This is a very common rabbit hole, and some credit unions never escape back to strategy again.

In reality, your experience, or that of your daughter, or neighbor, or complaint letter, may simply be one anecdotal tale. It is usually a symptom of nothing, just a bad day or a miscommunication. Could it be a red flag? Should such experiences be investigated? Absolutely, but just as complaints are invariably forwarded in all service areas, the Board's only roles regarding the complaints are to ensure there is a valid and effective mechanism to deal with them, and that those methods include trending to discover if there's a bigger issue.

The Board member from Hell (whom I describe later) used this all the time:

"Well that's a lie," he would say to one of my Executives, usually the current Head of Member Experience, "because here's what happened to me."

Or my personal favorite:

"As Chair, I can tell you that I have been receiving an unusual increase in member complaints."

Here's the thing about that last statement. Not one Board member asked how many complaints there were, how much the complaints had increased, nor over what period of time that they were received. At the time of that particular statement, the credit union had just gone through a banking system conversion, and had well over 100,000 members.

I commented that I had received only about half a dozen actual complaints over the past six months. He responded that he had either dealt with them himself, or that he had passed them along to the Member Experience team. When I checked with the MX leader after the Board meeting, the response was that there were a few, but no significant trends or increases above normal…even with a new banking system change.

So, I checked on net migration from our credit union over the previous few months, I checked on our growth in overall accounts, dollars, and memberships. All were positive. There was simply no evidence of this being a serious or trending concern.

Now, having said this, all negative member experience should be taken seriously. That is how you establish yourself to become top in the field, so we were meticulous in ensuring complaints were addressed wherever possible, and even the irritating, anecdotal stories in the Board room were, by habit, followed up on and addressed.

Board members like this will simply exaggerate the anecdotal in order to fan flames and support their case to get involved in an area where they feel they have the answer.

It is not, nor should it ever be, a process for the Board to get in up to their elbows and make wild and unsubstantiated 'member experience' judgements, or directional changes. That would be building a solution (often costly) without even exploring whether a solution needs to be built. They are rarely statistically confirmed as a negative trend. They are usually simple anomalies.

Yet Boards of credit unions jump into this fray time and time again. I posit that it is ultimately due to the lack of expertise and the resulting knowledge insecurities of the Board members. Most are in a position where they just do not understand the sophisticated challenges presented to their role, but can really bite into those they can relate with, so they throw their passion into those.

I cannot tell you how many times that a treasury decision, or a commercial lending decision of significant value ($20 million plus) were passed in a Board meeting within a few minutes, while the fact that a Board member didn't get a call that his/her GIC was maturing, or had to wait on the phone for 7 minutes ("because I timed it" they say), became an *hour-long* discussion— eventually forcing an in-camera meeting to discuss Management's apathy over these extremely important member experience issues.

I have also experienced some brilliant Board members that are well skilled, stay strategic, challenge intelligently and professionally, and are very valuable partners as a result. Unfortunately, after 44years with over 22 of those years in the CEO seat, these are the exceptions in credit union land. Credit union Boards are responsible for billions of dollars of trusted funds, and the majority of Board members are just not skilled enough.

In my opinion, the only way to improve this process of electing credit union Board members not being skilled enough, is to have the government that regulates these entities force them to have three approved experts appointed to each board; a lawyer, a CPA, and the organization's CEO. Without those three areas of expertise making up a strong base on the Board, the current lay-board makeups of many credit unions across Canada will continue to hold back their organizations. They take the regulator's view as gospel, which has been clearly evidenced to be lacking in its own expertise and yet very much subjective (which makes the latter statement extremely concerning); or the Board members fear what they cannot comprehend and therefore are 'safer' to simply decline the proposal— not a good decision-making filter.

Boards need the ability to hear all sides of every decision to make and support good resolutions, and I have seen too many boards leave CEO's out of discussions (in-camera), where one or two board members can, and do, make unprovable, often anecdotal, statements to sway other less experienced board members.

The CEO is the Board's chosen advisor, and yet because of the private sector experiences— which are a completely different mandate and environment— CEOs are never considered a real part of the credit union's functioning Board… and they should be.

This ensures the Board as a whole can only function with that expert advice registered in the decision process. When you consider the lengths and depths of lay persons that sit on these Boards, and how one dominant (often mis-informed) lay Board member can influence (and sometimes bully) other lay members; one might wonder how they even function without that insisted expertise on the Board as a built-in safeguard already.

I doubt whether this recommendation could ever be implemented however, as the private sector believes CEO's are too manipulative (totally different mandate however) and that appointments of the same, are not the purview of government in this environment. Which if you think about that argument, is pretty counter to its actual mandate of protecting member's interests.

As it stands, it takes tremendous self-discipline amongst credit union boards to ensure the appropriate expertise is at the table and that NO decisions are made in-camera before thoroughly discussing with at least the CEO for the very fear that they haven't heard all sides of an issue. In some cases, those previously described 'dominant' Board members don't want others to hear "all the facts" or even counter positions to their own. This has and will continue to compromise the process for good decisions.

"Once the facts are clear, the decisions jump out at you."

-Peter Drucker

Unfortunately, most will not have that self discipline and too many Board members misinterpret Governance responsibilities.

Boards are there to Govern the organization, not to operate it and not to hold onto some theoretical democracy flag that ensures the everyday person's perspective isn't forgotten - I call this credit union snobbery. A kind of motherhood position that protects ignorance and lack of relevant skills or experience; and ultimately works against the overall good of the organization and the membership. It is designed to insulate unprepared or unskilled Board members by establishing a value to the fact that while they really have no idea about the business or the mechanics of the business other than being consumers of its services, because they provide the member's perspective.

Think about it; if this is the main criteria for Board members meant to Govern sophisticated financial companies, it is a recipe for ineptness. I don't mean to insult Board members of credit unions but if they really have the best interests of their members at heart, they too would want at least half of their Governing Board to be highly skilled and experienced. And they are mostly not.

The fact is that in most and I do mean <u>most</u> credit unions, you're lucky if 10% of your total membership use their democracy to vote for Board members and/or resolutions that affect the operations and Governance of their credit union. Even less go to the AGM to check up on the organization; and only when something riles the employees do you really get members taking much action at all.

This leaves some very important and, in some cases, critical decisions left to a small group of members, most of whom simply do not have the expertise to make those decisions effectively unless they are determined to avail themselves of that expertise – mostly through their CEO. It also opens the door for small groups to at least 'theoretically' kidnap their credit union. Unions, employee related groups, friends of current Board members, even family members of Board members. Yes, there are some safeguards on the most blatant of these attempts but there are (and have been) very easy ways to circumvent those safeguards.

In one case a credit union had very strict rules on "campaigning" and even disqualified a potential Board candidate when he was found to have sent emails around soliciting votes from members and most specifically the credit union staff. At the very same time, in the closed Union halls, those Union backed candidates were trumpeted in meetings and Union members holding membership in their local credit were told in no uncertain terms to get out and vote for these 'Union' candidates; it was even outlined in their published newsletter. What was the difference in turning a blind eye by the Board and nominating committee? The Union candidates were incumbents.

Choices: Your Life is What You Make It   *Kelly McGiffin*

Choice: *Real leadership is more important than whether it's you leading*

Choices: Your Life is What You Make It   Kelly McGiffin

Choices: Your Life is What You Make It   Kelly McGiffin

Members of credit unions do believe in the value proposition that a cooperative financial institution has a dramatically different profit model that by its very existence should be a more humane and community minded entity. There are simply no small group of investors or employees that will be greatly advantaged (to the extent of a private enterprise) more than the organization itself. It's just not possible, so the Board should only focus on the life and sustainability of that entity.

    I had a similar argument in my capacity as a Director of a cooperative association that I sat on the Board for. I've found that "Cooperators' are extremely protective of not letting non-cooperators (and they define that as those not currently dedicated to cooperatives) on the Board.

    I found that disturbing. In my mind, the Board should have leaders and influencers that can assist in Governing coops in their mandate, which is to assist many groups in taking their destiny into their own hands, right up to providing poverty-stricken areas to find ways out of poverty through credit union micro-lending or cooperatives developed to raise their business games.

One board member even suggested that some wealthy people, that might help on the pragmatic side, could enter that Board with an agenda to compromise the cooperative organization for their own benefit. I asked him, how could they even do that? The mandate itself determines who that coop is. Change the mandate and the entity ceases to be; it would be a leap to suggest someone would see that as an advantage of any kind.

Yet he and others insisted that the risk of that compromise was worth keeping the Board pure with cooperative people first. In this example I would argue (and did) that the sustainability of the entity was being jeopardized by the Board's own misguided demographic value.

They went as far as saying, that Bill Gates himself wouldn't necessarily be the right fit for this Board. He just wasn't a cooperator. Like or don't like Mr. Gates but I challenge anyone to really think twice about not permitting him on the Board of any coop or credit union. Cooperative or credit union snobbery seems like more of an insecurity issue than applying a logical concern.

Governance is a key issue for companies today and while the government and particularly the academia of business have carved out a great deal of traction in trying to assure that governance is uplifted, (not to mention a little hard cash niche for governance education) following the Enron (often cited) debacle and the crash of 2008; the fact of the matter is that great companies are NOT built by great boards. They are built by great CEO's.

Any board that thinks they have that much influence on the company's operational success track is delusional. The Governance 'EXPERTS' taking your money have a self-interest in promoting Board importance – it's the core of their business model

– educate Board members and exaggerate their importance thus ensuring they want and need education and assistance in the role.

The only decision that a Board can really influence significantly in the direction of building a great company is in hiring the right CEO and allowing that person to lead the company toward greater performance. And the follow up to be a partner, collaboration team, second set of eyes, is where their real value is. Understanding that takes courage, faith, support and yes, checks and balances. Boards can keep bad CEO's in check but they can also keep good CEO's from full functionality, and if boards cannot distinguish that line, they are more dangerous than good.

Choices: Your Life is What You Make It   *Kelly McGiffin*

Choices: Your Life is What You Make It   *Kelly McGiffin*

Lesson: *Life's Not Always Fair*

Choices: Your Life is What You Make It   *Kelly McGiffin*

Choices: Your Life is What You Make It   *Kelly McGiffin*

As a manager and as a leader, the one constant that haunts those that seek to control and fix all situations, is that life is just not fair sometimes.

My dad was always trying to make me tougher, a real boy, a man's boy. One day he brought me home a puppy, a mongrel that clearly was mostly cocker spaniel, so not going to be a big dog, but not a little 'yapper' either. Every boy needed a dog, that was just how it was. I took to it right away and "Puffy" became my first true pet and I loved her.

Now a few years after we got Puffy, and after Kirk got his own dog, King (a German shepherd mix), my dad invested in two pigs to raise and slaughter; sell one and live off the other. It was his first attempt to provide more for the family. We had the room, and Tapley offered one of his pen-and-fence areas to raise them. My job was to feed them, twice a day, clean the shed of their mess (if you know what I mean), and keep an eye on them, make sure they didn't escape, etc.

One day, coming back from town, I immediately went out to feed the pigs. They would usually scurry out from the shed or under the shed as soon as they heard me coming, as they knew it was usually feeding time. If they didn't come right away, I just banged on the food bucket and they'd coming running. Not today.

The pen was vacant and I feared they had somehow gotten out. That was big trouble, as the pen bordered the forest and the pigs could be lost for good. I went on the run for my dad and he ran out to look. Sure enough, he found them huddling under the pen, afraid for their lives, and when he coaxed them out, one was bleeding and missing an ear.

He called Tapley over, who happened to be home, and discussed what might have happened. My dad thought it was a cougar, a wolf, something like that, but Tapley suggested it was likely the dogs, as a cougar would not have given them up and gone under after them and there were no wolves in our area, ever.

He insisted that now that they (the dogs) had tasted blood, they'd be back after them. He insisted that my dad had to get rid of the dogs and by get rid of them, he said clearly, "you have to shoot the dogs".

I was 8, and I immediately broke down. He couldn't just shoot Puffy, she was my dog and I loved her. My dad nodded and called a friend of his over that owned a rifle. They took the two dogs out, and while I threw myself at him begging him not to take my dog, he solemnly looked at me and said,

"I'm sorry son, I have to, those pigs are so important to the family and I have to think of the family."

I understand that more now than I did as an 8-year-old, but I wonder if that truly was the only option. I also wonder how I might have handled the same situation when I was a father.

I ran up the stairs to my bed and sobbed and cried as I've never before or since. Never, either, have I been as heartbroken, as I think a young boy or girl's heart is much more emotionally fragile than that of an adult. For the next few minutes I knelt by the bed and prayed with my entire heart and soul to God that he spare my dog.... until I heard the shots. At that point I was inconsolable and literally sobbed all night, praying to God that somehow a miracle might happen.

In the morning when I woke up, I made my way down the stairs, still heartbroken. My dad was still in bed as this had been a Friday night event and it was the weekend. I heard a noise at the door and when I opened it, God had answered my prayers, there was Puffy. Muddy and panting, but wagging her tail and jumping up on me. No, I wasn't dreaming, somehow, they had missed her and she had stayed away all night. I was now crying with happiness and joy.

That was until my dad got up to see the dog and said,

"Holy shit, we must have missed it. I'll have to call Don and go back out with her."

I couldn't believe my ears, I screamed that he couldn't, he just couldn't, and that this was a sign from God. He just looked at me and shook his head. He grabbed the dog, put her in the car, got Don, and did it right this time. I've never had a dog since.

Lesson here: life is not fair sometimes and you'd better be able to move on. We just cannot control every decision made by others and no matter how much we believe we have a relationship that will influence those decisions, sometimes they just don't.

Real accountabilities come from the willingness to think about our actions AND the consequences of those actions; whether intended, like protecting our family from losing a valuable asset like those pigs, or unintended, like a further lifelong deterioration in relationship with a son.

You may be doing the right thing given all the short-term facts but have you really thought about the long-term and perhaps unintended consequences? Self awareness and self assessment should not be disparate partners.

Choice: *Choices should be based on Lessons*

Choices: Your Life is What You Make It   *Kelly McGiffin*

Choices: Your Life is What You Make It   Kelly McGiffin

On the CX front, my thoughts went along these lines; credit unions in Canada have long been much more highly rated for their service levels, going back several decades to the point that those superior service reputations are now taken for granted by credit unions…and an argument can be made that this fact of historical service superiority is waning.

In a recent IPSOS Best Banking award feature, while credit unions were first in overall CX and branch experience, banks surged ahead in friend and family recommendations, rates and service charges, product and service excellence, and online and mobile services. In addition, the banks were ahead in value for financial planning, advice, and technology.

How long can a credit union afford their service reputations to stand (mostly unchanged in decades) above the competition as things change, especially in this ever-evolving technological environment?

I started to question how different our CX really was. I know and have met many people in banking and some are every bit as nice and dedicated to their customers as those in my own organization. So how do I know we offer a different level of CX?

I was trying to think about our CX and a concept for reframing CX in a financial services context. I struggled with how to consider setting a new bar. Many other FI's had looked at Disney, retail outlets, hotels, etc. yet none really ever made a significant move forward. There were plenty of good ideas, such as new branch experiences, utilizing big data to develop trends, creating new customer relationship management software programs to assess the big data information, etc. But none had really set any new bars, they were all just variations of what has been done the same way for decades.

Know and call the customer by name if you can; smile; friendly eye contact; look for opportunities to upsell or cross-sell; refer them to another service when they have questions; keep track of conversations and clues for next time; and make sure you tell them: "Have a nice day."

Choices: Your Life is What You Make It   Kelly McGiffin

Choice and Lesson: *Envisioning a New Level*

Choices: Your Life is What You Make It   *Kelly McGiffin*

Choices: Your Life is What You Make It   Kelly McGiffin

About that time, I headed out on a vacation to a resort in Nuevo Vallarta with my wife, Denise. We had not stayed at this resort in the past, but we found in our research that it was a well thought of resort, all inclusive, on the beach, and had good ratings.

    Our arrival was not disappointing, the resort was beautiful and like many of the other well-researched resorts that my wife had booked us in over the years, it was awash with luxury settings. Marble floors, spacious lobby, inviting exotic drinks as you entered, service that was outgoing and accommodating, and a scenic backdrop of the ocean waves crashing onto the sandy shore beyond a pristine pool area and lounge chairs edging the walkway to the beach.

    The rooms were pretty nice with two double beds, tiled shower, sliding door to the outside, larger tv, in-room fridge with a few beverages, very comfortable indeed for a week's rest and relaxation.

Upon our arrival we were of course offered a free spa treatment and $100 hotel spending, should we take a short tour of the complex. We knew this was a timeshare ploy. We were experienced travelers and knew exactly the schtick being used. I said to my wife, let's do it, we have three days before the rest of our group arrives and we have time. Let's get the perks— we know how to say 'no' and have before; she agreed.

The next day we met at the appointed time and were given a drink in the lobby while we awaited our tour guide. He was young man, very polite, and spoke very clear English, which helped this Canadian couple. He gave us the lay of the land and explained that the offer they were hoping to show us was a condo experience in their sister location, the Residence.

We were clear that we likely had no interest but agreed to at least head over for a look at the other property. We were about to be amazed beyond expectation.

When we entered the Residence, the lobby entrance was a similar layout to the Resort, large lobby leading out to a beautiful pool area. The difference in finish however was palatable. The marble seemed smoother and glossier, the pool water seemed bluer, the chairs more comfortable, and when we were led into the lounge and given a drink of our choice, even the liquor was clearly richer.

We met there with a new guide that lead us to the rooms being offered in this condo purchase. The room we entered was without exaggeration, perhaps the nicest resort or hotel room that I have ever been in. Walking into this spacious two-bedroom suite, with full kitchen, dining room, living room and bath, master suite with walk-in closet leading to large private bathroom and shower. There was a full deck overlooking the Residence resort and out over the ocean, you could see that most rooms in the resort were very much the same.

Then they led us to the rooftop private cabana and infinity pool, designed for all penthouse rooms. Denise and I were not expecting this much of an upgrade and whispered to ourselves, even at our income level, this was likely unaffordable but the tour did its trick and piqued our interest.

My wife is a great negotiator, she won't admit it but she is. I'm sure that its because she's cheap (don't tell her I said that out loud, but its very true). If she's going to spend money, she makes sure she gets what she expects out of it, and this event was no different. She was ready to walk when they presented the opening price, but by the time we left, we left paying exactly 85% less than they originally wanted…yes, we got the deal for 15% of their opening bid.

She also ensured the week and a half left were all given to us by shifting to the Residence from the original resort and that the other members of our party were given the same VIP access that came with Residence membership (in all parts of both resorts), as our guests. Further, the deal included a cash refund annually should we agree not to book in peak times (Christmas, New Years, Easter and Holy Week). The refund could stand to pay back the total principle spend within four years of the fifteen-year agreement.

We paid cash for the deal and once paperwork was completed, we were shifted from our 'comfortable' room to our penthouse suite in the Residence. When we checked into the upscale resort, our plastic wristbands were cut and we were given braided wristbands (with a metal resort logo entwined) that gave us VIP access to restaurants and beach locations that regular guests could not access. These offered better food options, premium drinks and even the seat cushioning was superior. The level of VIP service at the Residence itself was so upscale that they had an ice-cream unit come by the pool area daily, servers that would come by to offer to clean your sunglasses without having to request it, and even a guy that came around to offer a citrus water spritz to help cool you off and improve your tan while in the sun.

The point of this story is that I thought a lot about this example and how it related to CX in my industry. Every FI that I had witnessed had similar levels to the first resort. They had their own version of marble floors, pristine pools, and tropical beaches, but were indistinguishable from one resort or bank to another. Some might be slightly better in one area or another but all in the same quality level overall. Yes, there were, and are some that don't rise to that level at all, but near the top has become very much the same from bank to bank.

We felt that way about resorts, it's the reason we chose the Maraval. It was our assumption that a good reputable resort had a certain delivery level, and that they would all be pretty much the same and very comfortable, meeting that rest and relaxation goal easily attained.

However, we had no idea that there was a level above that, far above that – a place like the Residence. And in our industry, no one has defined that next level. And if you don't know there's a next level, you resolve yourself as a customer that you're at the best level already; which works great for the FI's that haven't done much more than tinker for decades. But what will happen when a next level is invented and then discovered by customers?

Company pride has many FI's (banks, credit unions and others) thinking they have that level above, but I don't think that's true, and I would challenge that sentiment to the point of experiencing the boast for myself. Happy to be surprised but likely won't be. And the opportunity therefore lies in inventing that next level. And I believe it is a major opportunity.

If you think about other such examples in other industries, it isn't a stretch to remember when WestJet, in Canada, reinvented their approach to flying for customers several decades ago— lower fares, less rigid approaches, jokes on the plane, priding themselves on the experience. These were quite radical departures from the CX of the airlines of the day, and WestJet quickly carved out a very successful niche. Today, they are hardly different however, and many customers have gone back to Air Canada, who had to up their game…and did.

That industry has now gone back to much the same from airline to airline, and only if you fly internationally and experience some of the Asian airlines or Air Emirates type of CX's do you see or feel a palatable difference. I anticipate that someday those examples of differentiation may be incorporated somewhere in North America and again carve out a niche for someone, introducing that next higher bar.

The challenge as I thought this through was and has been, how do we establish this new level for the financial service industry?

Choices: Your Life is What You Make It   *Kelly McGiffin*

Choices: Your Life is What You Make It   Kelly McGiffin

Lessons lead to Choices: *Using Life to Understand People*

Choices: Your Life is What You Make It   *Kelly McGiffin*

The Mexico experience gave me some thoughts to draw upon, some rhetorical questions to ponder.

- We were clearly amazed that there even was a new level, so how did they know how to build on what was already a great level in order to build it?
- What was it about that next level that attracted us to spend the money to move up when the current level was already pretty darn good?
- What were the core elements that we (and clearly others) related to?
- How and why did that successful offer also ensure price flexibility for the provider?
- How would offering such a level reside and be prepared in this age of internet and less interaction?

Exploration of these questions led me to some observations based on my own experiences and basic instincts that I believe I share with most people.

In the modest success that I've had in my life, I firmly believe most of it has come from my ability to relate to everyday people in our society. As you've heard from a few of my stories, I've struggled, had some adversity thrust upon me, had to work to make good choices, understandably grown up with some insecurities, and had my values challenged regularly.

As a quiet observer by nature, I revel in watching people and trying to understand where they come from on issues, and why they behave in certain ways. I have no formal training in this observation experience other than my sincere wish to understand and therefore use that understanding where I can to assist and/or serve.

Ultimately, my goal was to succeed by helping other more talented or gifted people succeed. Perhaps the insecurity of not feeling I was overly blessed with any real talent, drove me to find a different way to succeed but whatever the underlying reason, I have become adept at trying to uncover core drivers.

In CX I have a theory that there are four basic human traits in all of us that can be and need to be leveraged to create strong CX foundations. As a huge Beatles fan (growing up in the sixties), I best remember these traits through song titles.

1. 'Eight Days a Week'

I believe most people want both immediate gratification and want it as often as they can get it. As digital service becomes more and more prevalent in lives, this trait escalates. How quickly do we want responses from others over social media, how quickly do we want to hear news, how often are we checking that medium to see what's going on? These expectations for quick information are not lessening as they fulfill this new need, they are escalating those needs to faster and faster expectations.

If we are going to build that next level in CX, we need to understand this as one of the traits that is now nothing more than table stakes. We need to ensure our customers get answers, services, and access; 24/7 and lightning quick. If that is not built in and very reliable, our services are not going to be next level.

And this means available when they want it available, and in a format that they want it in. Gone are the days of bank hours and gone should be the days of predicting the access and pushing customers toward one access or another. Consumers are now the drivers, as they have many more choices for all services, at good prices, varying levels of access and speed.

They want branches, they want telephone, they want internet, they want payment services, they want international access, they want to able to use other devices, apps, etc. Our focus should be in having our services available in every format, not invent one that is better.

I sat on a National Payments Committee for the Credit Union system a few years back and left the committee after witnessing the group struggling with how they would compete with Apple Pay, or PayPal, and other disrupters that were predicted to disintermediate our customers (members).

The bulk of the discussions were focused on building or experimenting with payment systems that could offer members access that would be competitive with such entities. I felt at the time that we should not even be spending time or money on such options. We were not a payments company; we were a cache company. Our role was the vault not combination. We were the television, not the VCR, Beta or DVD player.

The way I saw it was "as the television" (TV), our challenge wasn't how customers wanted to access entertainment, it was to provide a base that allowed them to use our TV in any format they wanted for access. We needed to become 'smart' TV's that could plug in VCR's, DVD players, Apple TV, Netflix, etc.

This is from a blog by a young woman, Sara Azmoudeh, in an article titled:

The Instant Gratification Generation.

"Adults over the age of 50 will jump to say that the younger generations are lazy and have no work ethic. They pride themselves on their 100-hour workweeks with no breaks, their long walks to school and their written letters to loved ones. They tell us how much more interactive life was when the cell phone was put down at the dinner table, and "Facebooking" didn't exist. They preach to us how the true essence of fun lies outdoors, and not in our rooms with our Netflix and video games. Times have obviously changed.

Or are we just more efficient?

We are the generation that is contingent on instant gratifications. Now, what does that mean? Well, in short, "We want what we want, and we want it NOW." While that is contrary to almost everything we've been taught-delayed gratification-we have an

But how can you blame us?

We do not remember a time without microwaves, iPhones, instant hot water, Facebook, Myspace, you name it - we got it. We live in a day and age where you do not have to leave your home for ANYTHING. If you want the newest, coolest restaurant's sandwich delivered to your front door, the app Post-mates has you covered (not to mention, they have competitors, so you've got options). Through your fingertips you have access to all the world's information - so why even use a book, right?

It does not matter where you are, or what time it is - if you need to get home (or anywhere for that matter), Uber has your back with the ride.

The iPhone has an app for almost everything your heart desires. I mean, you can even buy a new wardrobe, and meet your significant other, online, at the same time.

Now this culture, like all things, has two sides. People either reach a false realization that everything in life is instant and easy, or people become more efficient.

And when people are used to getting what they want AND they are more efficient, what happens...?

Innovation is a part of evolution, and that is what has contributed to our culture of instant gratification. Behind all these products and devices are people from this generation - and ideas. Ideas that were executed and are now coined. I would argue that the older generations are wrong. The instant gratification culture has indeed burned the appreciation for strenuous work, yet the amount of ideas and opportunities it has bred into society is evident. People may not have to work as hard in all aspects, for while they may still have to push themselves in some, they will be efficient in others.

This generation still has to work hard, just in different ways. Perhaps the instant gratification they have learned and adapted to has instigated a sense of perseverance. It is not necessarily that *this generation will try, and when the gratification is not instant, they will give up. Rather, they will try and try again until they can make the gratification instant."*

The perspective that Sara expresses is likely quite enlightening for most of my generation; and remember, we make up a large portion of the CEO's and Board members for many organizations.
And yet, hers' is the generational demographic we all need to succeed with now and into the foreseeable future. It confirms that CX in this day and age has to include *"We want what we want, and we want it NOW."*
If this approach is not baked into the formula of your CX, you're doomed before you start. And unfortunately for those building the new CX models, this also means they want what they want, want it now, and want it HOW they want it; whether it be to walk into a store, access it online, over the phone, through an intermediary, physical delivery, etc.

Eight days a week is not even an exaggeration in this first trait and never has it been so critical to understanding the wants of customers. The generations" priorities and expectations have changed and a successful CX build has to accept it.
Gone are the days of manipulating customers to fit what was the most efficient and cost-effective way for the retailer. Banker's hours were great for the bankers. Weekends off were great for the employees. But as consumers demand more and more, we either adapt or let our competitors do so.

2. <u>Help</u>

The second human trait that I believe is unalterable is the "Can you do it for me?" trait. Help, I need someone, can't you please, please help me?

Perhaps it goes back to some of the comments in Sara's blog and the conditioner that prepared a new generation of consumer to grow up and become; but it seems like when the going gets tough, the tough just call for help these days.

I worked as a CEO for about half of my management career, over 22 years in total and I do not know how I survived without an Executive Assistant. She made all my travel arrangements, right down to directions to the car rental, rewards pre-built into the travel use, list of restaurants I'd likely enjoy when visiting another city, and a detailed agenda of whom I was meeting with, times, places, and topics.

In my office, she ensured my supplies were loaded, booked my appointments, and built in reminders to keep me on track. She put together special dates to help me remember key personnel's birthdays, anniversaries, and even some family notes on kids, spouses and hobbies for each of my key contacts. (I have a terrible time remembering names, very seldom forget a face but names fly out of my head).

She kept notes for me at most meetings and even gave me advance weather reports for driving into the office. I came to rely on her on a daily basis and while the reliance was great, at the same time it bound me to loyalty for her. How would I have survived without her in this job? And it would take an infinite amount of time for a replacement to learn the nuances of my quirky management and preference habits.

I don't think my enjoyment and ultimate reliance on my EA would be an uncommon one, given our nature as humans. Most of us are brought up in loving, protective environments where our parents (or in some cases at least one parent) does everything for us. Makes our meals, washes our clothes, drives us to events, and so forth. We're kids, so of course this is the way it has to be but it also sets a base comfort level when someone 'takes care of you' that is almost instinctively preferred.

While its healthy that our parents also try or sometimes force us out of this comfort zone, I believe that the basic (I'll call it) instinct to rely on someone else to do the stuff I don't really enjoy, is always there.

We've been fortunate to witness recent AI attempts to fill this void with devices like Alexa and Google Assistant but also in developments even before that with voicemail, electronic calendars and prompts, etc. Anything that can take care of tasks that allow us to free up time and, in many cases, extra work.

From a CX perspective, the ease with which we want to accept helpful help and our natural affinity for such, shouldn't be considered as a judgement or deep psychological issue that we need to study, rather to simply to explore as a base for building a CX that is most likely to resonate.

Is there a human being alive that wouldn't want the luxury of an executive assistant on a fulltime basis if they had that choice? And if you built your CX so that every customer had that kind of experience, felt like your company went that extra mile in their delivery of service to them, and was helpful and proactive on your behalf, do you think it would escalate that CX?

The thought of customer advocacy and agency is not a new concept but in this age of sameness in the CX world, perhaps it needs to be considered more deeply. What are the kinds of things that your business could offer your customers that makes their life easier, more time effective, or takes care of things for them? How do we become truly helpful?

And as happened in our young lives, that likely dependency on the truly helpful becomes both trusted and must be taught to give up, thereby standing a very good chance of long-term loyalty to the brand that best builds it.

3. <u>Baby You Can Drive My Car; Yes, I'm Going to Be a Star</u>

    We all want to be special, it's what drives us at almost every level. While most of us band together, birds of a feather and all that, uniqueness is a primal need.

    People get tattoos, color our hair, grow long beards, listen to music too loud in their cars, make a scene in public, many different tactics to draw attention to themselves. This is nothing more than our need, even if only from time to time, to draw attention to the fact that we are individuals. Notice me in this moment.

    There is no feeling like that of being a VIP, for an evening, an event, or a lot of the time. We strive to score the most goals, to drive the nicest car, to live in the nicest house, get to the top of the shop at work, sit in the best seats, fly business class, or just find a way to get our few moments of fame; modest or extended.

    Ever see some of the celebrities of the world? Some are not attractive at all, yet seem to have the most attractive partners imaginable. Is it their money that attracts them? Or their fame? Likely both because if they were your average Joe or Jane, they likely wouldn't have that attraction without one of those two things.

    This may sound harsh or superficial and I'll be the first to admit that most of those people may be excellent people without looks, and that should attract all people. Who you are SHOULD be more important than how much money or fame you have but we all know that is not how these things happen in the real world.

    And I am simply an observer here, I am not making judgement. The fact is that people will do a lot, and give up a lot, to either get that fame and status, or get close to someone that has it; hoping some of it will rub off or that by association they create their own uniqueness or modicum of fame.

We clamor for autographs or selfies with celebrities, maybe for memories or for purposes of showing our appreciation for their talent – at least that's what we tell ourselves. Or is it to post those 'accomplishments' on social media and/or show our friends that we had that moment of contact that they did not – making us the envy of the moment.

Again, not judging but in the context of CX, it is extremely important to understand why people instinctively want to be the VIP they admire, even if only for moments.

When I was born my dad insisted that I was to be named Kelly. It was a stretch in that day and age to name a boy Kelly and I was never happy with the name as a boy. I was teased a lot that I had a girl's name and I asked my dad about it early on. He said that Kelly was a fighter's name and that he wanted his boys to be tough enough to handle life. I guess it was a Boy Named Sue kind of thing. It did not sit well with me then and does not to this day, in terms of the reasoning.

I was not tough at all, I was quiet, studious and rather timid as a boy. I was very shy and found it very difficult in social settings (still do). My dad sensed that, and at about six years old, he decided to teach Kirk (then 5 – who by the way was named after Kirk Douglas, my Dad's favorite actor who just happened to have that tough guy persona) and I how to box, so he could help us protect ourselves as we grew up.

My dad's constant influence was always in the background. When he wasn't drinking, he was really a great dad. He'd tell us tall tales, he'd play guns with us, he taught us to play ball, and he would treat us very well. But when he started drinking, he became totally self-absorbed. He was never intentionally mean to us kids, never raised a hand but didn't have to, he was just plain scary and often inappropriate and uncomfortable. Not in a physical way but in his verbal communication, jokes and vocabulary.

Choices: Your Life is What You Make It   Kelly McGiffin

I had heard his friends talk to and about his toughness for years. Grown men would say to me, your dad is one tough son of a bitch Kelly. I saw him.......blah blah blah. I believed it all but more because I'd seen glimpses of it. He was never one to take an insult or allow one to any of his family. In some ways, he was a pretty fierce protector but a damn scary one.

The first time I saw his rage was with friends at our place in the country. He had called a few buddies over to help build a rail around the front porch of the old house. He was the worst handyman I have ever seen. I mean I am no carpenter either but he would make me look like Mike Holmes. Anyway, his buddies had a clue and finished the job.

Afterward, as always, they were drinking and the main carpenter guy (don't recall his name) took exception to something my dad said. He knew my dad well and retorted with some insult that somehow struck a nerve. My dad stood up and the guy said, "Look Bob, take it easy, I'm not going to fight you, I know you can kick my ass." My dad had this look on his face that's hard to describe. His eyes were kind of glazed over, terrifying really and his head would hunch over a bit, bottom jaw and teeth would protrude slightly, and he looked not only like he didn't care what the guy said, I don't think he could hear him.

My dad moved forward and the guy picked up a hammer, threatening to use it. My dad just lunged at the guy and both went sprawling through the new rail and off the porch. I don't know how he did it but he punched the guy in the face as they went over and when they landed, the guy was out and my dad was on top of him, just laughing. He got a cup of water, threw it on the guy and when he helped him up, they both started laughing, and went back to drinking. They never did fix the rail again and that porch just stayed that way until we moved several years later.

One of the nights I watched the kids, my mom came home alone. In a way I was relieved because when my dad came home too drunk, he'd always climb in with us boys (we shared an old brass bed in the upstairs bedroom – a converted attic) and he'd have us lie on either arm and cuddle us and talk nonsense for hours. In a way it was great because he was our dad and the warmth and protection was fantastic, especially for me as I had been terrified being alone all night but the non-stop talk and babbling that went along with it, got old and sometimes scary (how he was going to divorce my mom, or run off somewhere and send for us, or whatever else passed through his drunken brain). And most nights we both (Kirk and I) just wanted to go to sleep.

This night he didn't come home...until the morning. When he came home, we kids were just finishing breakfast, and I always felt an emotional dread when he came home. He could be so volatile that I just didn't know what to expect. It's a horrible feeling when you have a pit in your stomach, awaiting your father to come through the door at the end of a day.

In fact, for years when my own kids were growing up, I'd often ask my wife if the kids dreaded me coming home from work or not....I would have changed my life completely if she'd ever said, "kind of" or "sometimes" but she always seemed to make me feel like they loved seeing me come home. This was an important confirmation for me, daily. And my follow up was to put everything down when I walked through the door and give them some love and pay attention to them as soon as I came home.... every day. Still do with my grandson.

Anyway, he came home this one morning and both my mom and I could see that aforementioned look on his face as he brushed passed us all and went into his bedroom.

My mom rushed us kids out the door and told me to take the kids to play. I gladly abided and we headed toward Tapley's. It wasn't 20 minutes later that my mom called me back, only me. She said,

"Kelly jump in the car, we have to go get your dad".

I obeyed and got in the car.

"Where is he?" I asked.

"He's walking to town, something happened last night and he is walking into town to kill a man. And I'm sorry son, but you may be the only one that can get through to him."

She was now sobbing.

I was petrified...

"why me? How was I going to stop this raging bull bent on killing some guy? And why? What had happened?"

We pulled up to him walking down the gravel road about a mile from our house, middle of nowhere. I jumped out of the car and ran up to him from behind, yelling

"Dad, Dad, Daddy!"

Finally, I caught up to him and I just stood in front of him. He stopped but his icy glaze was shooting right past me. He didn't move, just ground his teeth, seething like an enraged animal. I yelled again.

"Daddy, what are you doing? You have to stop!"

He just stared. Finally, I walked up to him, all 9 years of me, and I took both of my fists and I hit him as hard as I could on his chest two or three times. I was crying by this time and didn't know what else to do.

He seemed to wake up out of his trance and as he looked down, he just seemed to melt into my dad again. I looked down and saw him drop a rock from each hand, carefully selected even in his trance to fit snugly inside his fists to ensure damaging blows to the guy he was after. Crisis averted... this time.

I don't know what happened the night before, I heard it was some kind of prank that embarrassed him and when he woke up, he was enraged with the prankster, and after a ride home from another friend, he was determined to teach the prankster a lesson. The guy never knew how lucky he was to have his life saved by a nine-year-old he'd never likely meet.

When it came to 'toughening us up' he worked with us every night, put us on a skipping rope program, and we ran one mile for conditioning, every day. About a year into the 'home' boxing program, my dad met Mickey Todson, a former European Championship boxer (German I think) that was opening a boxing club in town. He immediately made arrangements for the two of us to join. We had to go for an evaluation.

We entered the boxing hall Mickey had set up in the basement of a union hall and Mickey came right over to talk with us. He picked me out, saying Kirk might be a bit too young but he'd take a look at me. He had me show him on his hands (holding them up as targets) what my jabs and footwork looked like. He gave a tight-lipped nod and said, "Listen I'm going to put you in the ring with my son to see how you look sparring."

I was ready to wet myself. I thought, *"What the heck? You want me to go in and get beat up by your son?"* I remember thinking, *"Clearly his son is well trained, he's Mickey's SON. Oh God, I'm going to get killed!"*

I looked up at my dad, who had this big grin on his face, full of pride and I looked Kirk, who's eyes were wide open looking at me and he just shrugged, like – well what you gonna do? He was right, I really had no choice.

I got the practice gloves on, the head gear and stepped in the ring. The boy on the other side, looked polished and prepared and *not* worried at all. Mickey got in the ring and said,

"Boys you're going to spar. Richard, don't take it easy on him, spar as normal. Let's see what Kelly has. And Kelly, just move and jab like you showed me. Try to anticipate Richard's moves and counter or attack."

He started us and everything went quiet… in my mind. I have always been amazed at how focused boxing made me. Every time the opening bell rang, I went completely deaf. It was the weirdest thing I've ever experienced in sport. I believe it was fear in its primal stage and yet it served me very well from that first moment.

I started moving and jabbing and there was something surprisingly easy in seeing his punches, leaning back slightly as he threw them, having them fall uncannily short of their target and instinctively and immediately coming back with my own jabs that hit him.

I did this so well in this first session, that I rocked young Richard beyond anything Mickey thought was about to happen, beyond what my dad hoped was about to happen, and certainly what Richard had expected to happen.

I immediately became Mickey's prized pupil and he took Kirk as well, because the genes had to run deep in this boxing family. On one hand I was proud, and certainly my dad was over the moon, but on another, I was nervous. How many times would have to do this— fight another person… even just for practice?

Well the answer is about 7 years, until I was about 14, and it was 7 years of glory and pain, pride and dread. While my dad thought it made me more of 'a man', I hated it. I loved the training and hated the competition.

Having said that, it was likely the only sport I truly had a natural talent for and even my mom loved to watch me in the ring.

I was a boxer not a brawler and while I could move and strike as well as any kid, I truly hated the confrontation.

My time before bouts made me think of the story that I'd heard about Glen Hall the NHL goalie that used to get physically sick before most if not all his games, even well into his career. Prior to the competition, I was so stressed I doubt I could really function; and I'm still convinced that fear was the base of my successes.

However, the celebrity I gained in my own little corner was exhilarating. I fought through the anxiety and the fears for many years, not this time for my dad's approval but rather to help fuel my own ego. I loved being viewed at school as that boxer kid.

As a little guy at school, I literally never got bullied. I had two important things going for me. I was quiet and I had that reputation as a celebrated boxer. The fear of those unknowns kept people at a distance and yet, made me feel pretty special.

Ultimately it was outweighed by the panic and stress of the events, and I wandered away from it, looking for other outlets to stoke my status.

As an aside, my younger brother became a star in the sport in his own right – big surprise. He was as tough as they came at his age and size, and won more events than even I did. He always struggled when sparring with me (two different styles) but thankfully we were different builds and never actually had to face each other.

The point is of course, that we find many ways to bring a light to shine on our lives and we will often pay unusual prices to do so. If we really think about this from a CX perspective, it means we should be attempting to assist our customers with feeling that VIP status as often and as flagrantly as possible.

When my wife and I walked into that Mexican resort upgrade we were immediately jettisoned to a new VIP status and we've never looked back.

A few years ago, a colleague of mine heard I was taking the family to Disney in Orlando. We were treating all our kids and all our grandkids to a week in Florida, in what we suggested was a one in a lifetime family trip (at least once with us paying the shot).

He said that he had taken his family to Disney a few times and that they had discovered a VIP experience that was expensive but on an occasion like this, we might want to consider it. We checked it out.

We investigated and booked the tour for our last day. In a shortened description, you book a family or group VIP tour and Disney provides you a personal Guide for a day that is at your disposal to get you in through a back gate, front of the line for all rides (as many times as you like – your choice), special viewing areas for parades and events, and gives you some background and history of the park.

It's expensive and likely only an event you'd want to book once but we thought it was easily the best day we've ever spent at a Disney attraction and we've been many times. We're a big Disney family.

The most rewarding was the VIP feeling of the day. Getting special treatment and enjoying the experience of that special treatment, right down to the looks from others, was worth every penny. The CX versus value of that expense was worth it for us, and clearly for others. In fact, we've done it again since.

The key for us is to do it that last day however, because you're spoiled after that. "What do you mean we have to stand in line?"

Finding a way to constantly give your customers that VIP experience can make your CX stand out. But the challenge is in doing so consistently. If you are able to construct it, the value is very negotiable and may build more profitability into the loyalty quotient. People will pay more and yet want more.

4. <u>I Want to Hold Your Hand</u>

People need to be able to access all of their senses, if they wish to, in order to ensure a full CX. This is one of the conflicting values that have organizations wishing to keep costs down, relying on the superficial recognition of statistics that see online and mobile services escalating at rates unlike any such trends in history. They see a trend that allows them to both meet new consumer demand while also reducing staffing costs – ChaChing!

However, as a proud and eager shopper myself, let me give you some examples of why I differ with many experts about the need for human or sensory interactions to be built into your CX.

I love baseball, I mean I LOVE baseball. I played at a young age, much to my dad's chagrin as he was a big-time hockey player (top flight junior, and later a semi-pro in his prime), but I just found a connection with baseball. I read about baseball, collected baseball items, watched baseball and played at every opportunity; right up to this date playing old-timers baseball. And almost equally, I love shopping.

Maybe the shopping comes from my poor background and never having the ability to buy or get much at all, that I've been trying to catch up the rest of my life but I really like to shop. I'm meticulous in my appearance and my choices of wardrobe. Again, likely an outcome of insecurities and background but let's not go there on this subject.

I shop a lot, whenever I'm bored, even if it's just window shopping. I'll go to shopping malls and walk around looking at my interests; men's clothes, sports apparel and any sporting goods shops I come across. And if I find a baseball memorabilia store or baseball-oriented sports shop, goodbye for at least an hour.

Even as a baby boomer, I still have found a way to shop online quite effectively and have become the household expert in Google research and eBay shopping. As a result, I have no hesitation looking for items and ensuring that I have a great idea of what they cost and where I can get them the most reasonably. I also have very little hesitation in shopping online, even from China (albeit rarely). My experiences have been quite positive.

But here's the thing that I think most consumers, shoppers, will agree with. I will never shop for certain personal items, i.e. baseball equipment online. Even if I know the exact dimensions of a bat (length, model and weight), I have to feel it in my hands, feel the balance, inspect the grain, etc. The same with a glove or a helmet. Over the years I've simply found slight differences in each model.

I'm the same with clothes; they're just consistent in sizing and are especially difficult to really see how they actually look on me when I try them on. Seeing clothing on a model, in a picture, or just on a rack, can often look differently than we envision, once we try them on.

The CX of many products just are not fully appreciated or satisfying or even trusted without tangible touch. Even in CX designed not to have human interaction and targeted for a technical experience and bought for a technical experience, many companies have found they've needed to allow for human interaction to deal with some issues.

ING bank, one of the first banks to offer services of entirely online experiences, with the premise that their staffing cost savings could and would be passed along to those consumers willing to keep interactions as electronic, found that they eventually had to offer some branch locations to deal with people that needed to ask more questions and interact. And a recent study revealed that a major part of the consumer market had trust issues with FI's that had no branches.

Chat lines and phone services still need to be a vital part of many online offers in order to satisfy consumer's that have issues. Many younger people that have never seen life without a smart phone, are simply lost when that smart phone doesn't deliver as they'd hoped or been accustomed to.

When my own children went to University and College in the nineties, we set them up with online accounts through President's Choice which was banking offered through Canadian Superstores and partnered with the Canadian Imperial Bank of Commerce (CIBC). Even though they'd grown up in a credit union household, this service was online, offered zero service charges, and could be accessed on campus. All things credit unions did not offer at that time.

Invariably, each of them ran into some problem or another and when their frustration peeked without reaching one human voice, all three of them ended up with a traditional banking relationship.

They were all inclined and continue to use mobile services for almost all of their banking but I would suggest that none of them would do so without also having the option of a human to assist, should they need it.

While there are many apps out there and web information on almost any topic, including what seems like limitless YouTube videos to walk you through any area you might not understand, it is still much easier for customers to be able to call, chat or go into a place of business and have a real interaction when sorting through complex issues (for them).

It's the reason Apple stores continue to offer not just sales but expertise, classes, and guidance to users. Brilliantly, they still sell and upsell in the process, but there is an unspoken need to complete the full CX by ensuring there can be interaction as the customer wants, and again, when and where they want it.

I was at a seminar on CX a few years ago and a data expert made a presentation that was very telling to me. I don't honestly know if the data or the conclusions are the same today but it's worth reviewing the discussion that took place at the time. He noted that his research indicated that the current Gen Y, the most tech savvy of any generation in the history of man, were actually the generation that used bank branches more than any other generation.

He concluded that this trend, as surprising as it is, was because they were also the most financially illiterate generation in history. So, when something wasn't simple or simply understood through their mobile resource, the easiest alternative was to go for help in the branch.

Summary of the four human traits that I believe drive a great CX, are as follows:

1. Eight Days a Week – CX has to provide service to consumers when, where, how and as often as THEY want.
2. Help – People want things done for them and will not only pay for that but you'll create loyalty.
3. Baby You Can Drive My Car – There is nothing like believing you are a VIP, deliver that experience and you'll have people stuck to you.
4. I Want to Hold Your Hand – Do not discount or dismiss the importance of the human touch, the comfort and the trust for having it when they want or need it.

In determining your full strategy to address CX at a next level, I truly believe you need to consider these four areas to determine that your offer will really resonate with real people. Theory and practice are often divergent, working out scenarios to test using research, your own data points, control groups, and to make sure you're building a fulsome experience.

Creating a great CX and moving your business to a new level, above the crowd will take creativity, imagination, it will take strategic thought like never before, courage to plow new ground and invest in your vision and most importantly it will take discipline to see through the stages of implementation.

I don't know where my last credit union landed after I retired following my initiation of this new two-pronged strategy, or whether they took those ideas and moved them forward as had been planned; it was a daunting project with multiple layers to be considered and ultimately built and many leadership groups would not have the resolve or the appetite. I would not be surprised if they didn't lean back on the traditional 'follow the leader model'; much safer for new leaders.

I can see that the new financial model introduced has shown extremely good and positive results in the early years but I believe the ability to escalate CX to a new level continues to be a struggle.

Choices: Your Life is What You Make It   *Kelly McGiffin*

Choice: *Leadership Is A Choice*

Choices: Your Life is What You Make It   *Kelly McGiffin*

If a strategy fails or falls short it is often due to poor or unfocused implementation. This includes the tendency to give up when early wins are not forthcoming or early failures turn your initial courage and conviction into fear of failure.

    Be very aware, those around you will always have less courage than you will, when you are the leader. It is another human trait to want to sidestep failure and an easy choice to blame someone or something other than yourself.

    The whole team is with you when you win but a few losses and their often ready to point fingers and/or look for a new team. Don't be fooled by your own tendencies surrounding loyalties, many others are loyal only while you have value. This is not a jaded view but rather a realistic view that is forwarded so as a leader, you can better stand by your convictions and make the decisions that you know in your heart are right to meet your vision.

    It is a wise leader that hears and listens to his/her colleagues, and if you create the right environment, they will speak their truth and have their convictions. But it is a poor leader that doesn't contextualize those opinions. They should be kept in a place that is consistent with good decisions. The input of others is there to ensure you have considered all options and all possible outcomes, good and bad. Never make the mistake that such decisions should be made by consensus however.

If a decision goes sideways, as the leader, you are the only one that will be held accountable. Your Board, your customers, your employees, all stakeholders will have expected that you had the power to go in a different direction and if that direction fails, it is on you and you alone.

Your colleagues will rarely stand up and say, "Hey, that was my/our idea and I/we talked the boss into it." Of course, when things go well: "You know, that was my/our idea."

It can indeed be lonely at the top.

That's why the status quo sometimes seems the safer route, except it rarely is in businesses, as the world continues to move on. If you do not reinvent and ensure relevant value as lives change and therefore your value changes, your customers will move on.

Leadership is the most fascinating topic that I've ever considered. It is unique in scope and example, and yet similar for most in many ways. Every leader is unique because each is an individual with his/her own personalities, ego, insecurity, strengths, values, perspective, experience, life lessons, and influences. Yet it is similar in that expectations from leader to leader are the same. Honesty, integrity, intelligence, courage, empathy, caring, humility, drive, excellence, experience, consistency, and on and on.

Now we all meet those lofty expectations in different ways and to different degrees and yet those of us that have been successful in any right as leaders, also aspire to be better in each of those expectations as we reflect on our leadership's successes and failures.

I don't believe any leader sets out to be a poor leader, we all want to be great leaders and are confident that the judgement at the end of any of our given tenures is one of admiration, or at least one of high regard. However, there are many foibles encountered along the way, some that catch you by surprise, some that are ignored even for the flashing lights, and some are placed there dubiously by others.

Choices: Your Life is What You Make It   Kelly McGiffin

School Lessons: *Focus*

Choices: Your Life is What You Make It   Kelly McGiffin

As we grew into our teens, Kirk and I grew closer and closer. We're very opposite, and Kirk was always the more outgoing and socially successful of us. He was better with people, better with girls, better in sports, was extremely entertaining and charming, and always clearly my dad's favored child.

I was never envious of Kirk; I loved and still love him as my brother, and my best friend. And that devotion as a brother has taught me that you can enjoy someone else's success without envy if you open yourself to their well-being over (or at least equal to) your own. While I've garnered a modicum of success in my own right over the years, I know that Kirk has never had a moment of jealousy or envy. We are proud of each other for who we are, always have been and always will be.

The one thing I was very good at, and thoroughly enjoyed (unlike boxing), was school. I loved it. I loved the structure in terms of its continuity; the creativity within subjects like English, Creative Writing (different by the way), and History. And I excelled in many parts of school. I hung with a few other 'nerds', and school gave many gifts to those that like to keep to themselves when needed (the library is one of those).

I've always internally really liked people, the diversity, the difference in approaches, and empathized easily as I enjoyed trying to understand those approaches, perhaps more deeply than most. I am not good socially, however, and prefer to observe and appreciate rather than connect. This might seem like a contradiction. I genuinely love people, all people, and care that they do well, but I have trouble (without real effort) to socialize those feelings. I think that's why I leaned toward leadership in management and team sports. I could play the role that allowed me to show that I care without letting myself open to exploration by others. Better to be the explorer than to be explored.

On a practical note, one of the most important things I learned or adopted early in my school life was a habit of never procrastinating. While I have described this habit as being motivated by laziness, I wonder if it doesn't have more to do with ensuring I never disappoint others, and fast work leaves a lot of time to check and re-check your work. It's a great habit to create, regardless of your motivation.

So, what I learned early on was this; if you take care of those responsibilities early and thoroughly, you accomplish several things. First, getting the duty portion out the way both gives you time to review your work for real quality; finishing early in an evening or weekend creates more of your own time to pursue leisure choices; and perhaps most importantly, that time is totally unencumbered by any thoughts or dreads of the work not yet done. It seems so simple to me, and yet appears so foreign to so many.

The key is do the work right, and do it thoroughly. Throw yourself into it, double check its quality, and then you can put it away with a confident conscience. Don't compromise— focus. The real outcome however, is in developing a trust with others that you are someone that gets things done, and gets it done efficiently and professionally. Being a pillar of trust on any project has many benefits, short and long term.

This has been a hallmark of my work life and it has served me well as I've created the reputation of working quickly, effectively, and able to carry an unusually large workload. Really it is just time management, and what I believe is "laser beam focus".

Many years ago, I attended a conference, and while I don't remember the speaker's overall subject, he spoke about laser focus versus flashlight focus. It struck a chord with me both in terms of work and in sports. The speaker talked about how most of us have flashlight focus, most of the time. Broad focus that shines the light wide and thoroughly; it does a lot of good and keeps us on the path, and yet, at times, when really needed, we can focus that light (that thought) like a laser beam, intense and effective in cutting through problems and challenges.

It is impossible to have laser focus all the time, you'd burn yourself out, and many try, but if you can control your focused attention to bring out the laser approach when needed, you will accomplish much more in a short period of time.

That's what I tried to do; focus like a laser for a short period of a few hours, to bring the idea-flow, and logic structure to a project— at least initially, until I had a storyline that made sense and that we could approach more broadly. It worked and continues to work for me and I've been called both intense (can't hear a thing when I'm in that laser zone – just like boxing), and intimidating in the approach and the outcome (you've already finished the outline?).

Choices: Your Life is What You Make It   *Kelly McGiffin*

Choices: *Relationship Broken down*

Choices: Your Life is What You Make It   *Kelly McGiffin*

I didn't socialize well, but I did enjoy observing people and found a way to really enjoy them from afar. I still find observing people enjoyable, not from a judgement position, but rather from a really enjoyable appreciation for their diversity.

My relationships of choice were forged from this self-knowledge. Professional relationships were handled one way, social relationships another way, and personal relationships a totally different way. I keep them compartmentalized and effective for the most part because relationships in all their facets should be conscious choices, if you're sincere. I see the three relationships quite differently.

1. Professional Relationships:

Professional relationships need some distance and objectivity. As a leader, a colleague, and a coach, I need to intimately care about those relationships and their constant professional improvement in order for the relationship to be successful. No improvement in any parts of a person's life can be achieved if the whole person is not considered, so intimate care to know people is a critical factor in facilitating this.

In this relationship, I must consider their importance to me professionally but only in full context with how they are feeling about their role and how I can assist in them being the best they can be. Their value to me as their leader, as a colleague or as one of our players is only accentuated and fully successful if they are productive to the end game for us both or collectively (the team). If I am not cognizant of this, I leave a lot to fate and that's just not how I roll.

I really made this a focus as a coach, particularly with younger players. I coached in the Canadian Men's National (fastpitch) Softball Team program for about seven years, the last few years as the Junior Men's National Team Head Coach. During my time with the Junior team (19 and under), I realized that their egos were still forming and were much more fragile than seasoned men.

I needed to not only try to determine playing lineups, team strategy, and overall program development but in order to get the best from the team, I needed the best from each player. That meant ensuring they clearly understood the role I needed them to play on the team, that they were focused and ready for that role, and ultimately that I knew them well enough as people to be able to proactively help when needed. Not just as they went into slumps or struggled defensively but overall in their confidence, ability to focus when needed, and both up and down emotionally. This took a great amount of coaching dedication. In order to really know a person, you need to care enough to know that person.

I started to post a sign in my hotel rooms at every event:

"Care to care enough!"

It was simply meant to remind me that my most important job, if I really wanted to get the best out of people, was to make sure I knew them well enough to know how they were getting on every single day. The more I could read that temperature, the better I could assist, or in some cases, make better tactical decisions based on the resources at hand.

This approach also gave me strong license to make objective decisions. Because of this intimacy with people, there were not a lot of relevant conversations that were short-changed. If I needed to address a concern, I knew the tact needed and went about it with confidence.

Through this same journey, it came very evident that one of the most important facets of a professional relationship is that of absolute honesty. Many times, as a coach or a manager of people, the tendency is to soften critiques so as not to demotivate your charge. However, this approach usually ends up sending completely mixed messages, and the concerns you actually need to bring up are brushed aside as minor when they're really not.

This compromises both the charge in their evolution toward being their best, and the relationship in the end. They feel you're not consistent or that you're disingenuous with your discussions, and feel you're not telling them truth. People have pride in their journeys and want to do well, so if they are not hitting their stride as well as you expect or as well as you think they're capable of, why would you stifle or soften that help? But we do.

I found being straight up honest is easily the best policy, but it must be done in a positive and constructive context and has to be accompanied with either solid assistance that will help improve the situation or a willingness to brainstorm with them regarding ways to improve the situation.

Your job as leader should never include giving up on people. If you're leading them effectively, they will work until they either succeed in the role you need, or come to the realization that they cannot, and make their own decisions. Those that don't come that realization have, in a way, made those decisions and will force your decision. It is a decision that you will be able to make with good conscience, knowing you were honest, willing to assist and it still didn't work out. I never wanted to surprise a charge by letting them go and on the rare occasion that it happened, I felt like the failure.

This approach ensures a little distance to ensure any criticism aimed at performance improvement is objective and not personal. You know the person and you just don't see their performance as a personal failure or success…really. If they fail at winning a Championship, they may feel they've failed personally, but they haven't, they failed athletically.

Personally, they may still be great sons, daughters, partners, fathers, mothers, sisters, brothers, etc. As I've said to my kids time and time again; I want you to value yourself and others based on who you are, not what you do.

2. Social Relationships:

As mentioned, I am not a social person in any stretch of the description. Even after many years in the public forefront, I am very awkward socially. Painfully shy as a child, at most social gatherings, I'm the guy alone in the corner that has his wife checking in on him once in a while.

Never the less, I like people... a lot. I find them fascinating for the way they approach life, carry themselves, body language used, their responses and engagement in conversations. I can sit for hours in an airport, just watching people. Not in judgement but in analysis and amazement. People are quite fascinating and make this world a wonderful place.

Social relationships are important and I have to work hard to maintain them but you cannot care enough to care without opening that social relationship door. Therefore, the professional relationship is only possible with the social relationship taken into account, and in my case, cultivated beyond its initial awkwardness.

I discovered through my own experiences in having people show interest in me, that one of the quickest ways to connect with people is to take an interest in their most loved interest. This isn't a phony interest or parlour trick, it is that people have passion for things, and to get to really know them you need to try to understand and appreciate that passion.

For some it is as simple as knowing about or taking an interest in their kids. Almost everyone that has kids, can be consumed by their children's lives. It's what we do as parents. If you can ask about their kids, remember their names, what they're into, etc. you have not only a window into their hearts but a direct highway.

So, how do social relationships differ from getting intimate and knowing your players, colleagues or charges? Because the only purpose of a social relationship is sharing the enjoyments of a life well lived with someone else. There is no objective in a social relationship. You're not looking to make them better, or get anything from them, just share and enjoy.

These can be short term relationships, occasional relationships, and can sometimes lead to longer-term, personal relationships. They are critical to leadership though, because they give you that release of comradery without expectations.

Having a beer with your teammates, or dinner out with friends allow you an escape from the stresses of work, of family drama, of the influence of the world. It's 'play time' and it's critical to a healthy leader's rounding as a person. And while it has no real expectations, the habits and processes used to hone the social relationship skills play well as practice and foundation for the professional relationships.

3. Personal Relationships:

Personal relationships are deep, and require much more commitment than the others; not only in time but in personal investment. These are relationships that you would not think are highly relevant to a business career path but they actually are critical to it.

Family and friends, your true personal relations are your ground, your foundation, and if you put anything ahead of them, you will have regrets upon regrets.

When I first started at FirstOntario, a long-time Board member's wife passed on, and while I had never met her, I attended her service out of respect and affection for the Board colleague. As I entered the Catholic Church, I couldn't help notice how young the Priest was. As a guy that has long challenged status quo and therefore the 'power people' within a traditional status quo structure (i.e. the Church); I wondered very judgementally to myself – *"What was this young kid going to tell this crowd of mostly white haired listeners?"*

Again, I challenged (in my thoughts); *"typical Church approach, go through Seminary school and voila, you have the answers. And what's more pathetic – most of these listeners will believe you do!"*

Then, after the normal ceremonial processes, he began to speak. He said that he was young and couldn't know how it felt to be nearing the end, like some, but what he had done in his early priesthood was be at several death-beds and talked to many people that were nearing the end. Then he said something that I will never forget.

He said, not one of the people he comforted at the end ever mentioned that they had regrets about not living in a bigger house, or driving a better car, or not climbing Mount Everest, or even traveling more. If any of them had any regrets at the end, it was always one of the following: I wish I had been a better husband or wife; I wish I had spent more time with my kids; I wish I'd been a better brother or sister; a better friend; a better grandpa or grandma.

The only regrets he had ever heard at the end of one's days, were regrets around building better relationships. And even as a young Priest, he believed that this was the key to a life.

The place was silent and I could feel my heart swell. This was the most powerful sermon I had ever heard because it was so much the truth.

Choices: Your Life is What You Make It   *Kelly McGiffin*

Choices: Your Life is What You Make It   Kelly McGiffin

Lesson: *Life gets in the way*

Choices: Your Life is What You Make It   *Kelly McGiffin*

Choices: Your Life is What You Make It   *Kelly McGiffin*

I started working as soon as I was 16, the legal age to get my social insurance number back then, and that was needed to get a job. I worked at Zellers as a stock boy, every day after school and every weekend. It was not a great job but I got paid weekly and felt I was on top of the world. I could see the future end of my home life, which had been a dream since those long nights of babysitting in terror. I was going to save every penny and get out. That was a short-lived dream.

It wasn't long before my mom came to me and asked if she could take most of my pay to help with the family. She didn't demand, but rather explained that they were stretched in every which way and if she told my dad how bad it was, that she didn't know what he would do. Of course I would give it up, and I did. She did let me keep a few dollars so I was able to clothe myself in my choices, and that seemed to be enough for me at the time. My dream of escape would have to wait, that's all.

It is amazing to this day however, while I have always handled stress extremely well, and if I'm aware that stress is starting to manifest, I work out hard with weights or run on the treadmill. The sweat and exercise will always assist.

However, stress creeps up on us and I have found that I only know when I am at my maximum stress levels when I experience a certain recurring dream/nightmare:

I'm working and living at home with my parents again, and as I'm planning my rent for an apartment on my own, my mother comes to me and asks me to put it off and help her pay the family bills.

I invariably wake up in a sweat and cannot get back to sleep. Time for a big workout!

Of course, sooner or later, you do move out and on. My career took many detours and I'm proud to say that it started humbly and equally honest in admitting it was as much a stumble as a plan.

After a few more moves and upsets, my parents split up after my first semester of College. My mother finally mustered the courage to leave but not enough to take the kids, which now included a fourth sibling, my baby sister Jo-Ann (14 years younger than I am). Those she left with my dad, who hit the bottle hard and entrusted me to help with the younger ones.

I did my best for a year or two but clearly, an 18-year-old, even one going on 30, didn't have the tools to go for long; and the two younger girls went back with my mother.

Kirk and I set out on our own and he left high school to work locally, and still does. He's a hard worker that just wanted a simple life and to raise a fine family, which he did.

Choices: Your Life is What You Make It   Kelly McGiffin

Choice: *Choosing a Career*

Choices: Your Life is What You Make It   *Kelly McGiffin*

Choices: Your Life is What You Make It   *Kelly McGiffin*

I met my wife Denise in our home town. Three years younger, she came from an attractive family, and they lived in a 60's home in a 60's subdivision, drove the typical family car that was upgraded regularly but not lavishly, vacationed to Europe, Disneyland, etc.; the kind of family you'd see pictured in the 60's sitcoms—the likes of The Donna Reed Show, My Three Sons, or The Brady Bunch.

    Taking a leap of faith with a boyfriend clearly from the wrong side of the tracks was challenging for her family, and as her father described later, 'quite a disappointment' to him and his wife. In fact, he said to me,

    "You know Kel, when I met Brent (Denise's older sister Sharon's boyfriend and future husband– also over 4 decades together), I thought– oh Sharon, you can do better than that. Then Denise brought you home and I thought, oh my goodness, Denise, you can definitely do much better than that!"

    Now he quickly adds,

"Of course, I couldn't have been more wrong." But it did take him 40 years to admit that to me too.

Denise clearly saw something in me, I was neither the best looking of her options (she had many), nor was I the most charming, nor the most popular. We just clicked. They say opposites attract, and never has anything been truer than that with Denise and I. We complement and offset both our strengths and shortcomings for each other in all aspects of life, and I have no better friend in the world.

Finding the woman that I wanted to get serious with gave me my first real impetus to get my life on track. I went job hunting in the local mills to ensure I could support a life for us. In our home town's hay-days, there were three sawmills, a plywood mill, and a major pulp-and-papermill. Now, I hated the thought of working in the mills. Growing up it was the antithesis of my definition of success; but I also needed to be realistic about generating income and contributing to building a life.

I found work in the local plywood mill, pulling veneer sheets off of the dryer. It was not hard work but consistent, assembly line type work that paid very well. I resolved myself to the 9-5 type of role, and began to think about saving for a house, car, marriage, etc. I imagine it is how most of us start into a real life. Not exactly what we imagined growing up, but a compromise that moved us a little toward a general dream of home, family and comfort.

I think fortunately for me, the forest industry was very cyclical and about three months into this new reality, there was a massive layoff at the mill. I knew I had to scramble, and based on a short stint that I had worked at a Finance Company just before finding a real strong paying job at the mill, I expanded my focus to either laborer or entry level business.

Searching the want ads, I found that BC Central Credit Union was looking for an entry level loan officer for a small credit union in Quesnel. I thought, what the heck, I'll send in my interest.

I was amazed to be asked to drive over to Vancouver for an initial interview. It was at their BC Central's Head Office in downtown Vancouver, and Denise was just entering University at this time at UBC in Vancouver, so the drive wasn't unusual.

This pre-interview led me to my real interview up north in Caribou country, Quesnel BC. It was a good seven-hour drive to Quesnel, but I was on a path to finding a career to base a life on. I had some distant relatives there, so I knew I could get a little footing if successful.

I made my way up to Quesnel and interviewed on a Monday morning (office was closed as they worked Tuesday to Saturday) with the GM, Mr. John Quelle. I'll never forget John nor his wife Miep (the Treasurer of the CU) or his son-in-law the Insurance Agency Manager, or his son-in-law's brother, who was the controller. Yeah, you get the idea.

John was a very tall, older Dutch gentleman, very distinguished and very intimidating. He was looking for a young, moldable, future management type that knew a little about consumer lending (thank you, Pacific Finance), but not too much to have created habits he had to change. I seemed to fit the bill and he made me an offer during the interview. I was thrilled although I thought I blew it as I left…

He took me to the door to let me out and in his thick Dutch accent he leaned over and said very dryly and ominously:

"One thing you need to remember. I don't like to repeat myself!"

I remember realizing he meant business by his body language but I had one problem; with his Dutch accent, I didn't catch what he said and I innocently replied:

"I beg your pardon?"

As he repeated it, he smiled, clearly knowing I hadn't heard, but my heart dropped as he did so. I said,
"Oh I'm so sorry, I didn't catch that." thinking I had just blown my offer.
He smiled and said:
"You'll get used to the accent, its ok." …. Whew.

My time at the mill had me in a used 1970 Dodge Dart Swinger (more car than I should have been allowed to drive). Denise helped me load up my one suitcase, my black and white tv that only worked when there was a sock on the antenna, and a record player with my handful of albums to head to the new life.
Over the next 32 years in BC Credit Unions, I worked for six different credit unions—one with a repeat appearance—and I did just about every job one could do in a credit union, up to and including CEO in two organizations.

Choices: Your Life is What You Make It   Kelly McGiffin

Lesson: *Fired Once*

Choices: Your Life is What You Make It   *Kelly McGiffin*

Choices: Your Life is What You Make It   Kelly McGiffin

Denise and I were married early, she was 19 and I was 22. I was working in Quesnel and she joined me, but we both longed to go home, and as luck would have it, I got offered a loan officer job back in our home town.

I worked with our home credit union for the next seven years, moving up to my first Branch Manager job at 24, and leading the company in several sales categories for a few years at my first leadership post as Branch Manager, Ucluelet Branch. Our three children were born during this time, and when they were about 5, 3 and 1, the GM of our Credit Union called me in and asked me if I would take a transfer to the far Northern end of Vancouver Island and take over the branch there. I was flattered and off we went.

Little did I know, the credit union was in terrible trouble, and as a young Branch Manager, I was only focused on the Branch and my ability to lead the staff on its objectives. I found out later that the GM had overextended the organization in his drive for growth and diversity, and one of the first political moves I was ever witness to and eventually victim of, was the blame game. Today, Donald Trump has played this game like a master. When the light is shining on you and showing your flaws, redirect the light.

He had all Branches audited for irregularities and several of us were terminated for things that I look at, even today, and shake my head about. In fact, when he terminated me, this was his line:

"Kelly, if you accept this termination and resign, I'll give you six weeks severance, a letter of reference, and call a few credit unions to recommend you. I don't want to see your young family suffer."

What a great guy!

I had never so much as had a reprimand for any of my work and just the opposite, many accommodations, bonuses, and, clearly, opportunities. It was within a year that the Board came down on the GM and most of the senior team.

What did I learn? First, as I had learned before, life is not always fair, but even more so in business. Even in an ethical business like a credit union, you cannot underestimate the self preservation of people. My advice: keep your nose clean and your work record (the actual record) sharp. You can be terminated for any reason– many are not good ones– simply because someone wants to hire a friend, or because you're taller than them, or because of your popularity, or your talent threatens them, or because it gives them a temporary distraction.

But if your work is of consistent quality and volume, that quality will supersede their damage, as those that witnessed it will witness it for others. Your reputation will survive.

I signed per his request. What was I going to do, fight city hall?

He was true to his word and I walked into another job within a few days…in Vancouver, however.

Choices: Your Life is What You Make It   *Kelly McGiffin*

Choice: *Working up the ladder*

Choices: Your Life is What You Make It   *Kelly McGiffin*

Working in a major city was never my dream with young kids. I had grown up in a small town and I wanted to raise may kids in a small town. Being a Branch Manager was enough for me and it was 9-5, five days a week, good pay, and allowed me a leadership role within my community, and within my Branch.

    I yearned for a small town again, and one opened up within about six months, in BC's the Okanagan. We jumped at the opportunity and moved the family to Keremeos for the Branch Manager job there, and it was a little slice of heaven. This was my first tenure with Valley First Credit Union, and our CEO was Harley Biddlecombe, who would become my mentor, unbeknownst to him.

    I threw myself into the community and my family loved it there as they were growing up. We were living the dream for most families, making a good living, enjoying the community, respected within it, good friends, and every day seemed filled.

Then, in 1990 (the kids were now 11, 9 and 7), I was offered the GM job at a small credit union back on the Coast, in Powell River. I explored the opportunity, which was a flattering process for me at the time, but I didn't really take it very seriously. The credit union had some real challenges. It had just come off a four-month strike where the labor board closed its doors to avoid anyone crossing the picket line, and the aftermath of the consequences of the strike and the decisions made up until the strike were significant.

It was obviously a union shop, had one location, an in-house banking software system, no accountant or CFO type position, and was operating both at a loss and under Regulatory Supervision.

They offered me the job, I declined. They offered me the job again, with more money attached, I declined again. They offered me the job again, with even more money and I accepted.

This was a move fraught with peril, and one of the few times in my career where such a move was determined largely by ambition and ego. The offer was a good one, in terms of compensation, and anytime that is presented, it can easily stand to justify such a move in the 'family's best interest'. However, if I am being totally honest to myself, it was about the flattery and appeal of being offered a CEO position.

Either way, I soon found myself well over my head in Powell River and facing both personal and professional crisis. My family was uprooted, and Denise and the kids, while being completely unwavering in their support for me, really struggled with the move.

We bought an older house (one of the few available within our affordability window), and Denise's dad and brother made their way over from Vancouver Island regularly to tear it apart and completely remodel and update the house.

The kids were doing their best to adapt to their new home and their new schools. The two older kids struggled more, as they had to leave close friends, enter new schools, and were mostly viewed as 'outsiders' in this new small town but close-knit community. They adjusted after a short time, and while my heart ached for them, kids are truly resilient and what we learned was that for kids, if their family life is good, all of life is good. Engagement with them overcomes all such obstacles and they are all better people as a result, unafraid of any new community or environment.

On the credit union front, it was an unbelievably chaotic environment. As mentioned earlier, the Board I walked into was largely made up of Labour leaders within this Pulp-mill town. What I did not know was that the previous Board, the one that were in place at the time of the strike had all left the Board (one way or another), and the membership replaced them with this labour focused Board to ensure the strike was settled.

One of the first courses of action for this new Board was to terminate the CEO and close the doors of the credit union, so members were not put into a position of 'crossing' the picket lines to do their banking. This backfired on them, and as I walked into this new position, as green as a CEO could be, I faced a stack of Share redemption requests. This request is the formal request the members of a credit union make to close their accounts and get their initial membership shares back. As they were considered part of the capital of the credit union, they must be approved by the

Board to ensure their redemption does not compromise minimum capital levels for the credit union.

At the same time, it was evident that the credit union was staffed with a triumphant unionized group (they had 'won' the strike and were strutting their stuff); had an understaffed or at least under-skilled management team; it was in a loss position for the current fiscal; had a new and unfamiliar in-house banking software system recently installed; and no accounting position at all. Think about that last point. And unsurprisingly, was formally "Under Supervision" of the Provincial Credit Union Regulator.

I attacked the job with my usual enthusiasm and optimism; *I can fix this, that's what I do*. I really believed that the main course of action was primarily in rebuilding the trust within the walls of the organization. Initially I felt that turning the staff around and getting them working hard to re-market the credit union to their community would be the key to the turn around. It was a big part, but not even close to the extensive rebuild I found to be necessary.

I started with getting to know my team, really getting to know them. Who was who? What did they think of our chances within the community? What issues did *they* think still needed resolution to make this a success again? I also took the initiative to call every member within that stack of share redemptions to ask, no beg, them to give us a chance. There was a new Sheriff in town, and we were going to build the credit union back up, but needed their help.

These two areas seemed to click early on. The staff was ready to move forward and knew they had to work to keep this credit union alive. After all, it was no secret that we were under supervision, and that if we couldn't recoup and build business, we could be put out of business— out of jobs.

The members of the community actually really believed in a credit union. Ideologically, union towns not only believe in the credit union model, they often start them. The rub is that when the going gets tough, they bail.

Often, union members scream solidarity and brother and sisterhood from the highest soap box, until it affects their personal wallet. I've found that there are times when you just have to call them on it.

There has been many a good union participant screaming about staying out of Walmart because they are very anti-union; only to find that same participant, and most of their cheering colleagues shopping in that very same Walmart. Ideology is easy to espouse, not always easy to back up with consistent action. This isn't a slap at unions— it goes back to human nature. When it's your money, sometimes feeding your kids, or going on that vacation outweigh spending more on ideology.

In fact, in one of our very first Powell River strategy sessions, a Board member stood up and said,

"Kelly, be very careful about how you proceed. This is a union town, and they will not stay with us if they believe we're not doing things within their ideology."

I responded,

"Okay, but let's explore that. This is a predominantly union town and yet we, as the *ONLY* unionized Financial Institution in Powell River, are the smallest of all FI's. How is that possible? Secondly, if they leave us—what unionized FI will they switch to? Why do they hold us to a different standard?"

You could hear a pin drop.

The job that seemed daunting; rebuilding relationships both inside and out of the credit union walls turned out to be the easiest part. The staff wanted engagement and the community was willing to forgive, if not forget.

    The bigger challenge was in turning the credit union into a productive business… and it was clearly a bigger challenge for me than it would have been for many other well-prepared new CEO's— I was not one of those.

    As I mentioned; the organization had an in-house run banking software system— the whole engine of the credit union was within this system. I had only worked with systems that were run through third-party, outsourced service bureaus, and with those, if you had a problem, you made a call and someone fixed it.

    This was 1990 and we had just bought our first home computer. They weren't all that familiar yet to many families, and in our household, Denise was the expert on this limited early model. I struggled with the home computer, let alone an in-house banking system. And it was worse: no one in our organization had any background in this skill.

    Two of our more senior employees were taking a 'computer' course from the local college and had a checklist for backup runs at night, etc. So, they were valiantly making due, and hoping to learn more as we moved forward.

    I also was faced with financials that were not looking very strong, and I needed to understand where to head with this organization. In order to do that you must identify where the low hanging fruit is, in terms of both income generation and expense reduction. Pretty simple math. Except for one main criteria: you have to be able to read your financials in order to assess them.

    I had no accounting training other than a few basic accounting courses. We had no accounting-trained employees, and the same brave managers we had in place simply handed results to our auditor for accumulation. The Regulator, currently in a supervision role, was the best resource we had to help with assessment, but this was counterproductive to trying to get the organization righted and out from under this supervision— a key Board mandate.

Things soon came to a crystalized point for me, and forced me to make the biggest, and most critical professional decision of my professional life.

I worked long hours trying to wrap my head around how to take this organization forward, all while keeping a confident and upbeat presence within the branch and facilities for staff and members alike. I have long been a follower of two well known statements:

Anyone can steer the ship when the seas are calm.

Never let them see you sweat.

Leadership is about confidence as much as anything, but it is also about ensuring calm is evident when others are feeling stressed. "Its going to be alright" may be the most powerful thing a leader can state or, more importantly, show.

Heading home one night, I thought I should bring home the entire month-end books (actual printout spreadsheets in those days), the month-end that would lead to the organization's year-end. They were the numbers from the year just ending, a year that I had walked into just weeks before, so, while not my doing, they were my starting point. And the regulator had told me that they will show a slight loss for the year. I needed to understand why and how.

I sifted through the printouts at our dining room table, in the midst of a new home totally ripped apart awaiting the remodel finish. My wife and kids, and my father-in-law and mother-in-law (there to work on the house) had all gone to bed. I studied page after page of the spreadsheet over and over until they just looked like paper.

It suddenly came over me like a rush of fever. I put my head in my hands and started to realize that I had literally flushed my career down the toilet. *What the Hell had I done*? I was happy in Keremeos. My family was happy. I loved working for Harley and the crew, and I had let my ego get me into a situation where I was simply, well, over my head. I was on the verge of a total breakdown as I thought about what I'd done to my family.

I set aside the printouts and grabbed a cup of coffee. Even at this low point, I was not going to be my father and reach for a drink. Coffee made sense, as I had to figure out how to get out of this mess, it could be a longer night yet.

My stubbornness would not allow me to wallow, but rather determined me to stop thinking about poor me and think about the choices I might have to move my family forward. It came down to two choices:

A) Admit to the stakeholders, my family, the Board, and the Regulator, that I was over my head, and that we had both (the Board and I) made a mistake. I could arrange to stay on until they found the right person, finish the house and resell, likely at some profit (remodel); and call Harley to beg for my job back. He was very supportive (although clearly a little skeptical about my readiness to take on such a mess, as he put it), and there was surely a chance.

B) I could reach out to the stakeholders, the Board, the Regulator, the Auditor, and the staff, and be totally honest with all of them. I needed their help and patience in both giving me time to learn the stuff I needed to learn, and ultimately find the resources I needed to support me in this role. It would mean working closely with both the Regulator and Auditor in understanding the financials, and using them to teach me about what the numbers could tell me (us). It was a risky decision, as any one of them could simply make the same conclusion as I had, and force me into option A. And if it became their choice rather than my choice the damage would be much more significant.

I clearly decided on option B, and set about going back through the spreadsheets with a new perspective. As I read through them, I noticed that, on more than one occasion, some large payments were both made in expenses and again in accounts payable. Same amounts and same payee. First order of business was open up to the Board, then the Regulator, then the Auditor and ask them for help. Second was to ask this expense vs payable question.

The calls went exceptionally well, and frankly, I don't think I told them anything they hadn't already determined, but they opened their arms and set out answering questions and giving really valuable insights. And the expense/payable question was first order on the new menu. Of course, as you've all suspected, the lack of expertise had our people creating a payable for some major known bills, and then when the bills came up, paying them directly as expenses without ever drawing from the payable GL account. The discovery moved us from a slight loss to a slight profit. What a fast win, and while a simple and really not all that impactful move, it was a huge indicator to me, personally, that maybe I could do this.

Shortly after this momentous decision, our inhouse software system froze one late afternoon. The two caretakers could not find a solution, and it was so late in the day that they couldn't reach anyone from the software company (that sold the system, and had assisted with a few questions in the past). In brainstorming, they decided to call their College instructor to see if he might be able to help. He said he likely couldn't but knew a colleague, a little higher up, that he felt might be able to.

The college colleague came over right away, asked a number of questions, looked at the caretaker's, and played around a little until it came back to working condition. We were all very relieved, and I immediately thought, *"Well, maybe we have a resource"*. I called him the next day to set up a thank you lunch.

Lunch with Kim Lowcay went really well, and in getting to know him over the meal I also pleasantly found out that he was also working toward his CGA designation. He worked for the local college and was not highly paid (his words). This immediately planted a seed in my mind that he might have exactly the skill-set our little credit union really needed to shore up the two big gaps, IT and Accounting, right here in our back yard.

I immediately started to discuss making him an offer with the Regulator and Board. Both supported the need, and I followed up with an offer that Kim accepted.

First major move forward.

With expertise gained, at a reasonable local price, together we set out to learn and move this organization forward. The next two years were the most immersed I would ever be in my career, until I moved to Hamilton several years later to take over as CEO for FirstOntario.

I rolled up my sleeves, and read in detail the new freshly inked Credit Union Legislation; learned (alongside Kim) IT, Accounting, and Treasury; wrote and re-wrote policy based on the new legislation; established projections and budgets; and negotiated union contracts as they came up (first one settled in one day). Within those first two years, I learned more about credit unions and the operations of a credit union than I had learned in the combined previous ten plus years.

With this intentional intimacy gained, I was able to, and continue to be able to, understand credit union's cause and effects faster and more intuitively than most, and it's played extremely well over the course of the rest of my career. There is simply nothing like wearing all hats in a small credit union to truly prepare yourself for significant roles in larger organizations.

Outcome: we moved the credit union from $12 million in assets to about $60 million over the next four years before I moved on to my next CEO role. A few years before I moved, on I hired Dave Craigen to take over as COO, and take on the face of the credit union as we gained more and more community profile.

Dave was a local guy, looking to move back from the big city (Vancouver) to raise his young family back in his home town. He was a mover and shaker, and one of the most energetic guys I've ever known. The three of us were an unintentional dream team for a small organization, and when I left, Dave took over the credit union and moved it further down the line, further than we had ever thought it could go. I have always been very proud of him and his work.

Kim moved to Ontario to be with his kids after his ex-wife moved out there, and as chance would have it, Kim and I worked together at several other organizations, and do consulting together to this day on some projects. Kim is an excellent resource and an even more loyal colleague; I'm proud to call him my friend.

Relationships matter.

Choices: Your Life is What You Make It   Kelly McGiffin

Choice: *Learn from your Lessons*

Choices: Your Life is What You Make It   *Kelly McGiffin*

Choices: Your Life is What You Make It   Kelly McGiffin

In parallel, while raising three amazing children, I have a passion for baseball and fastpitch softball. I progressed from player to coach, to National Team coach, and back to old timers' player today in baseball and men's softball. I was a part-time scout for the San Diego Padres for close to 6 six years, and I appeared in several Provincial, National, and World Championships, as well as three Canada Games, and the 2003 Pan Am Games, winning Gold.

I've encountered challenges in parenting, (one of my children is bipolar and still struggles), career (fired more than once), and in coaching (the ego balances are unbelievable), and yet I believe that every experience has added to my insights.

If any one message emanates from this book, I hope it is that your life is what you make of it. We all have choices to make, and will go through many trials that can help mold those choices if you stop and learn lessons that come from those challenges.

You can choose to wring your hands and feel sorry for yourself because you had a rough upbringing or some bad luck, or you can choose to move ahead. In my opinion, we give far too much credence to poor upbringings. I certainly believe that there are damages that are close to irreparable, but often times we see fully grown adults still blaming their parents and upbringing for their poor lot in life. I think they have not made the choice to pick a route that, while perhaps more difficult, could take them to a better lot.

There are many such mantras like this:

- If it is to be, it's up to me.
- Only I can change my life. No one can do it for me.
- You can have results or excuses. Not both.
- Accept responsibility for your life. Know that it is you who will get you where you want to go, no one else.
- If you change nothing, nothing will change.

I choose to believe that all of these apply and I've lived my life that way. I've always told my children and now my grandchildren, if you don't like your life— change it. Don't wait for a lighting bolt from Heaven to touch your life and make it what you want, work to make it what you want.

This sounds like good advice, and an easy thing to help send kids on the path to a great life, but not everybody seems to be able to do this. I hope that through my relay of experiences, others (you) will have some better thoughts on the things you can and will do to impact your life (and ultimately other lives) positively.

The very first lesson in business, sports, and in life is to create your 'world of the future' in your mind. Don't allow any obstacles into this process, think about it and write it down, draw it, or just put to memory what you think would be the ideal environment for you.

If it's at work, is it the CEO job? Is it simply steady management work? Is it leading a certain type of division? Is it ultimately a different field?

If it's on the sports field, is it the League Championship? An individual accomplishment? A reputation for being one of the best?

In life, is it raising a family comfortably? Is it five kids, no kids, just a partner to travel with? Is it life in a big city, small community, tropical paradise, back in your hometown?

The hallmark of a life and career fulfilled is to remember that we are all just people, and life is much more enjoyable and satisfying when we judge less and enjoy each other more. Think about how pleasant your day is when you run across that one person that just makes you smile.

As we work toward our life aspirations however, it is the easiest thing in the world to let your ego get away from you. Or perhaps for some, it's less ego and more insecurities that get away from them.

It happens every day, and often it is nothing more than one person either putting down another to feel good about themselves (acting in a way that drives attention toward them) or just reacting to the emotion of feeling insecure.

It is so dangerous, and therefore so important to constantly surround yourself with those that can help with that awareness. It is the only cure!

If you cannot find that kind of cast, you need to be able to reflect on your own experiences that can remind you.

Choices: Your Life is What You Make It   *Kelly McGiffin*

Choices: Your Life is What You Make It   *Kelly McGiffin*

Lesson: ***Egos Do Damage***

Choices: Your Life is What You Make It   *Kelly McGiffin*

Choices: Your Life is What You Make It   *Kelly McGiffin*

When I was a very young boy, I remember driving into the city from our place out in the country. The three of us kids were in the back playing, as kids did in the 60's. No seat belts, a bench seat, singing and or playing on the 20-minute ride. We arrived into the hub of our small town and parked on the street in front of the Bank. My mom and dad were going in to see about getting a loan for a new car. Well, new to us, not really a new car.

    My parents went into the Bank and left us in the car, as was the norm in those days. They were gone a while, but not an unusual amount of time for a business trip for us, and when they got back into the car, my dad was visibly enraged. We all knew the signs, and as the oldest I sensed it and innocently asked why daddy was so mad.

    My mother turned and told me to sit back and play, that this wasn't time to talk about it. She knew silence was the order for the day now, and we did too.

When we got home, my dad went out the back to sit on the porch and steam, as he did to avoid losing his temper. I asked my mom again,

"What's wrong?"

She always treated me like the oldest and confided things in me that perhaps a mother shouldn't, but then she was only seventeen years older than me too, so how would she know.

It turned out that when they went into the Bank and met with the Bank manager (or loan manager or whomever the man was), they explained the need to borrow a few hundred dollars to get a new car as the old one was getting less and less reliable, and with three kids out of town, it was pretty important.

The manager leaned back in his chair and shook his head,

"How can you possibly even have the nerve to ask for a loan when your credit rating, and our experience with you has been so shaky? There's nothing we're prepared to do for you, Bob."

Even at a young age, I couldn't believe what she was telling me. I was not surprised that my dad had poor credit, and while I didn't know what credit really meant, I knew he probably was in rough shape financially. Heck we ate puffed wheat for breakfast, lunch and dinner most last days of the month. We didn't exactly have a pot to you-know-what in.

What I was shocked at was that this man would be so mean in his answer. First, because he was very lucky my dad didn't snap. But even more so, it struck me as mean, and while I didn't understand the terms at the time—demeaning and disrespectful.

I will tell you this. I remembered this story my whole career and reminded myself in dealing with every personnel issue or customer issue to never be disrespectful, and always wondered if the person in my office (who I had to give bad news to) had kids waiting in their car. I didn't take short cuts. I tried to give them alternatives, and I always made certain I treated them with respect and empathy. Every time!

Respecting another human being, regardless of their lot in life, should be table stakes. And yet it is not.

We so easily lean back in our chairs like that banker. Or we strike back when attacked;

"Oh yeah, well if they're going to do that, then we're going to do this…"

Understanding takes the time and discipline to stop and *seek* to understand. Only then can we hope to be truly respectful of others.

If you are going to be successful in a leadership position, it must be because you lead well, not just because you succeed. Winning is not always a sweet experience, and it is certainly not as sweet when your win is tainted.

Choices: Your Life is What You Make It   *Kelly McGiffin*

Lesson: *Ego's make you smaller not bigger*

Choices: Your Life is What You Make It   *Kelly McGiffin*

Everything you do as a leader counts, so it is my belief that when in doubt, try to do the right thing for the right reason.

In one of my CEO lives, I had **"*the Board member from Hell*"**. The worst Board member that a CEO can possibly have. You know the type, they know everything, and come in as a total bully in the room. They can talk platitudes about ethical behavior and are usually from a position of authority in their previous life (military or law enforcement, etc.), and of course have the market cornered on ethics and the law. And true to the nature of this kind of narcissist bully, he wouldn't allow a real lawyer, like in-house legal, to weigh in on areas he already had determined on behalf of the Board. If the legal resource had been asked to clarify, the requestor or the legal resource would soon be looking for new offices.

Even when he was proven wrong through a court decision, he refused to admit it. He would take the position that this was a radical change that had never happened before in the history of the law, and would definitely not happen again. The judge got it wrong.

He would insist on many in-camera meetings without any management to discuss almost every issue, so he could not be debated, or so facts wouldn't be presented that might cloud his claims. He limited management's input and warned us ahead of time what we could present in a case he didn't agree with.

He made inappropriate jokes, he demeaned and outwardly bullied management and other Board members, and his hubris even led the Board through what could have been litigious actions had the greater membership been aware, and yet he held tremendous power.

In fact, that's how he kept power; bullying and intimidation. When that didn't work on some of his colleagues, he bated them until the other Board members got tired of the battles and agreed to "payout the trouble makers" (an obviously outrageous approach to a democratically elected Board).

I worked around him mostly, appeasing his ego and carrying out the mundane little directions that he gave, that really didn't affect the operations of the organization. The good news was that he wasn't really all that bright and didn't have a good grasp on any of the big issues, so he was not actually an interference for me in my performance.

He knew, through our direct discussions, and through my constant correction of fact within Board meetings, that I did not agree with many of his positions or antics. We had a very poor working relationship based on his insistence that he was the boss, a position I challenged when constantly reminding him he was the Chair of the Board, and simply could not act alone. He knew this and conceded this often, and near the end of our time together, he started to present his position as *"the Board wants this or doesn't like that"*.

When I responded, "Ok then, I'll bring it up at the next meeting to reassure them of my understanding and discuss some adjustments", he would insist that it wasn't that big a deal, and I shouldn't fan the flames. I knew immediately, this was really only his issue(s), and as such, I did what I thought I could do without compromising my decisions on behalf of the company good.

Being a CEO is often consumed by that balance. Doing what you know has to be done for the company and its stakeholder; all while addressing squeaky wheel issues. Doing it well is the hallmark of a good CEO.

The sad part of this faux leader however, is that he was never self-aware. He thought he was both a great leader and an astute operator. I took the position that while he was Chair, I had two mandates: run the company (as CEO) / and appease the Board (him); and the two rarely overlapped.

After I left, he took the company in a totally different direction as he hand-picked the next leader, and was certain to choose one that would not resist his direct involvement and direction. I've never bothered to really look back but I speculate that this manipulation and ill-advised direction, including some very counter-intuitive actions, eventually resulted in significant need of repair. The ease of complete re-directions however reaffirmed two things to me:

1) Culture takes on the leader's values and can change quickly with a new leader;
2) Great companies are created by great CEO's not by great Boards.

Leadership is both a critical component for great organizations and a fragile trust. Your platform can be compromised by others through actions and for reasons that can range from simple ignorance of implication or conscious and nefarious agenda.

The values you espouse as a leader must be grounded in your personal values in order to have any chance of leveraging them as the most powerful tools in an organization. If you are faking them, or do not have enough self-awareness to realize that you don't really demonstrate the values you state; your sincerity is immediately (or, at the very least, eventually) questioned and your leadership is forever compromised.

Through my writing, I hope you've gained a glimpse of my values as a leader. For me, these are the tenements of great leaders:

1. Respect for people is the bedrock.
2. Do the right things for the right reasons.
3. Walk the talk that you expect.
4. Use strong and thorough analytics to make evidenced decisions.
5. Utilize creativity to tackle the real problem, not perceived ones, to ensure real solution.

The values of the Board member from hell that I just described would best be listed in this way:

1. You need to respect me.
2. I'm smarter than anyone else and my gut is always right.
3. Any evidence that contraries my opinion and might seep through to the Board was just fake news.
4. If you oppose me, I'll get you sooner or later.

Now, we know many leaders like the latter, that have been very successful, one is the current President of the United States, and they are successful by many standards. But not all success equates to being successful as a leader. Rarely are these types admired, only followed, and their eras, in retrospect, are almost always viewed as blemishes rather than successes.

I'm not suggesting for a moment that my leadership has been all success. I've made many mistakes, let my ego run away on occasion, and had more than my share of failures. But I do believe on the whole, I've tried to learn from those mistakes, taking real lessons from my failures, and have regularly checked my ego to ensure that I've been respectful and thoughtful with people.

I hope that my successes go beyond the statistics that normally measure such things; those of growth, profitability, stature, etc. I want them measured by relationships that are enduring and have continued, and that those relationships were clearly built on a foundation of mutual respect. I would like people to think of me as one that was a positive catalyst and a sound, strategic, and courageous leader. I hope they remember me with fondness, and that during my tenure they enjoyed their job, the company, and their overall involvement just a little more than they had before.

Choices: Your Life is What You Make It   *Kelly McGiffin*

Choice: *Care Enough To Care*

Choices: Your Life is What You Make It   *Kelly McGiffin*

When I was coaching at the highest level, I realized that in order to be the best you can be as a coach, you need to be able to unlock your team. To do that, you need to care about your players to the point that you take the time to know each player, respect their needs (from you), and adjust for each. Your job is not to get the most from them, but to get the best from them.

You cannot do that if your sole focus is on winning. When that happens, it becomes about you. *"We have to win, its my record as a coach"*. Suddenly you find yourself late in a tight game, pushing buttons and pulling levers you don't need to. When really the key to winning is keeping each player intensely focused, but loose enough to play well and let their talent out.

Ironically, when you push the panic button that you have to win, you're likely taking away from letting that talent win for you. You're creating a stressful environment that has them tighten up to the point where mistakes will be made. Reminding yourself to know how to get the best out of them, means you have to get to know them enough to know what they need in that moment... and they're all different people.

It is a very difficult job to do this as a coach, and an even more difficult job as a CEO or a manager. Often times, you're too busy in your daily life to stop and think in these terms.

I call this putting out fires all day, because that's what it feels like. Its an easy trap to fall into, get to the office as the leader and just let the day flow. Deal with all the little fires that are burning, and be a solution finder. It's satisfying, it's appreciated, and it's time consuming. And many leaders spend almost all of their career approaching the job of their leadership in this way, going from meeting to meeting, looking for, and often providing, solutions to daily problems.

Then once a year or so, they pull their team together to discuss plans and budgets for their upcoming year. I think most managers, CEO's, and leaders can relate to this process, and putting out daily fires is a very important part of the job. But think how much more effective you would be as a leader if you spent every morning, or even better, every day's end, evaluating how the actions of your day folded into, or helped shape, or contributed to your actual strategies for moving the company forward, or for your peoples' development?

I think it would start to shape or filter just how you viewed the next days activities as you started them. Every action would start to demand that you have context for it. Some of those actions would still be focused on a remote or unexpected fire, but even in putting that one out, you would start to wonder if that fire could have been averted, and you'd ensure the energy in attending it was contributing to the greater objectives.

I posit that most fire dowsing comes from flawed planning and preparation, and the only way that you will effectively know that is through review each day on what those fires were, and why they cropped up. If they're not fires that are actually part of the strategy, or fires we didn't anticipate, we can either start to eliminate them, or adjust our plan to allow for change.

The worst that can happen is a creation of management distraction, one that strives to meet mostly just to be informed, and double or triple check on process. This is flawed activity and can eat up a leader's time very quickly and unproductively.

In sports, there are four mindsets or mental stages needed to be successful. The first is the strategic plan in our heads. What is our plan to succeed, what do we need to do to be our best? This mindset is usually accomplished as we set out into our season and determine our goals, and reflect on what it will take to achieve them.

The second mindset is in preparation to succeed. Concentrating on practice, on repetitive mechanics to teach muscle memory, on raising our conditioning, on working on timing, on establishing protocols that will serve us well in the heat of battle. This mindset and work sets the stage for performance.

The third mindset is in implementation. This is *'the Now'* and it makes certain that we are thinking about only the simplest of activities to ensure absolute, laser beam focus. I describe being in *the now* as having successfully built stage two on the foundation of what was needed, that *now* I only have to stay focused on my implementation. The strategy and preparation for success has been done. You cannot be successful at implementation if you're mind is continually running back to strategy or preparation. The process for adjusting those thoughts based on what you learn through implementation is in stage four, the review.

The fourth mindset or stage is the review of the day's activity or performance. This is usually done by the athlete themselves, as they've either succeeded or failed at their activity in their opinion. If success was achieved, every athlete will still replay that success to ensure (they're very honest in their quest for perfection, especially at high levels) it was a result of their plan, and is therefore repeatable. If it was a failure, or even partial failure, they will immediately log it in their practise plan for the next day or session.

I'll give you an example; when hitting a baseball, I strive to get players in the *'Now'* as much as I possibly can. It is extremely difficult to hit a moving ball, especially when they are thrown hard and moving with different spins. If your mind wanders to anything but seeing the path of that ball for even a split second, you stand a good chance at failing on your swing.

Hitters invariably wander to thoughts about what pitch it might be (we call that guess hitting), or getting their foot down, or worse, driving in the run, getting a hit, etc. And I maintain that any thought that creeps in, other than "see the ball" will ultimately interfere with being able to hit the ball, which is the *ONLY* objective at that point.

How does a player let go of all those other thoughts? There are tools you need to work on, mental exercises are offered in lots of literature, and one of the best that I've recommended over the years is Heads Up Baseball by Ken Ravizza and Tom Hanson.

In business, it's about staying in tune with activities leading to strategic objectives. Every day, your actions intended, unintended, planned, and unplanned should be reviewed in advance and in reflection.

On the way to work: *What am I scheduled for today? What will I have time to tackle? What is the purpose of this activity and will it help in the quest?* At work, as the schedule changes, reflect on the value of the necessitated change. At the end of the day, reflect on the productivity and try to put it into a context toward the strategic goals.

Highlight the key accomplishments in that vein, and at the end of the week reflect on whether each day has worked and led to another step forward, or dealt effectively with removing an obstacle toward the strategic goal or vision.

Is this a discipline to develop? Can you develop it? Is it realistic to take that time to actually map the process and keep it on course? Yes, but you need to carve out reflection time; purposeful reflection time. Only then will you learn from your daily activity and train it to become more productive toward your long term goals.

Diaries and journals are easily the most effective tools, but to make them more about process than feelings they should be structured carefully and specifically to do so. I've included a rough template for the kind of journal priorities, headings, and format I used below. But it is easy enough to create one that is more specific for you, or for your operational team. Perhaps even engage a printing company to prepare 'company journals' to assist your leaders.

There are also a variety of websites that can provide more thoughts, research and templates for you to consider and initiate these valuable tools.

My personal journal format:

Vision, Mission and Values of the Company

Here I would list these (ours were succinct) to remind myself of the over-arching company statements.

My Strategic Focus

Here I would try to come up with my own key strategies for the present year, to ensure I was driving toward the company strategy. Even though I was the CEO, I would sometimes outline the current key strategies for the company, such as: 1) Diversify income sources and 2) Tangibly improve our member (customer) experience; and then my daily review of activity could easily be back-checked as to its relevance to these key company strategies. This kept my eye on the ball.

These two headings were specifically designed to remind me of the big picture, and were embedded into every page of my work journal.

Daily Goals

Here I would set just one or two goals for the day. Often on my drive into work, I'd set these in my head just based on the predetermined schedule. But I also often thought of a few other additional goals for that day. Interestingly, once I sat down to quickly jot them into my journal, I found reviewing the first two headings could force a change to the priorities or lead to even different daily goals. Its quite amazing how much a constant view on strategy can force a different perspective on managing your day as a leader.

Under this Daily Goals heading, I would usually try to indicate where in the schedule I would facilitate the time to accomplish them (often already in my schedule), as well as an expected outcome. Again, keep the morning notes brief, they are quick reminders not exhaustive plans. However, be sure to leave note room for the outcome of these meetings and activities. Ensuring you write your impressions, concerns and ultimately the effects of these activities, will drive their continued success or needed alteration.

The rest of the diary had headings without need for notes in the morning. They were designed as reflective note areas, reserved for the end of the day.

Unplanned Work

This was a heading needed every day to remind me that there are always fires to be put out and distractions are constant. They must be dealt with, but allowing for them, and reviewing them in the context of strategic focus allows you to better manage them and the amount of energy you put into them.

Important Lessons or Notes for the Day

Perhaps the most important section of the journal. Here you need to reflect on what happened this day. What worked, what didn't, what you need to consider in coming days. This is a wide open set of needs for your journal and should be kept as your diary forward section, if nothing else.

Personal Notes

Leave a section for your personal thoughts, distractions, and if you feel you have nothing from your own world, use it to take some time to think about your colleagues, superiors or subordinates. How was your leadership for them today? Remember in any leadership position, your relationships will dictate much of your success, so consciously think about it.

Conclusions and Action Plans Forward

Here is the summary and items you need to note for further action, discussion, consideration, etc. Stay on track.

Whatever form your journal takes— whether its self-made format, a completely different set of considerations than those in my example, or whether you are able to find or build one electronically in a software program— the importance of the tool is its ability to keep your balance between being in the *'Now'* and reflecting on that effort toward the big-picture objective(s). Without that discipline, most of us will spin wheels beyond necessity.

There is a reason that great minds like Einstein, Da Vinci, Edison, and Franklin kept work journals; and we're much better off that they did.

Choices: Your Life is What You Make It   *Kelly McGiffin*

Lesson: *Math is Hard but Simple*

Choices: Your Life is What You Make It   *Kelly McGiffin*

One of the final lessons I want to ensure future leaders consider is one of business basics. The math.

In business, you are selling something no matter what business you are in. There are a lot of semantics surrounding the word sale or selling, but at the end of the day, we are selling something for money. The key is in understanding *what* you're selling, and building the appropriate tools to do that well.

Most competitive businesses sell very similar products, and eventually services to the greater consumer base. Even the big companies like Amazon, Microsoft, Apple don't really sell things you can't buy elsewhere (delivery, OS, technology). What they really sell are their brands. Now everyone reads this and thinks, *"Duh"* and yet we rarely link this commonly held opinion/fact to our own businesses.

In banking, while we were selling loans, mortgages, savings accounts, etc., we were really selling the Financial

Institution (FI), not its products. With very little variation, every FI has the same products, so when you're selling to a customer, I think you're actually selling the FI and thereby its products, not the other way around.

Yet every FI focuses more time on pricing of the products to differentiate, than focusing on their brand. Even the big guys on the block will push brand for a while, and then onto product and price. So, if you really do agree that, your business value proposition is in establishment of your brand as the better choice, how much and how complexly tied is your brand to not just the spend, but also to walking the brand's value proposition?

If you agree with the premise that brand is what will differentiate you at the end of the day, you can start to really link the thoughts on leadership and culture. Your brand is almost entirely about how you do business. How you really do business is how you carry yourself when no one is looking; and that can only be truly qualified if it is built in... as your culture.

I have witnessed culture change dramatically and quickly based solely on a leadership change— both positively and negatively. As Brian Tracy famously said;

"Everything counts! Everything you do helps or hurts, adds up or takes away."

If you are a leader and you believe that counting nickels and dimes will turn into hundreds and thousands, that is how your culture will develop. Your customers will feel it, your differentiation will show it. I recently witnessed a leadership change in an organization where the new leader felt there was just too much wasted expense.

While he continually stated to all that would hear,

"We are not shrinking ourselves to greatness; we are going to find ways to save money and grow our business in a fiscally responsible way."

He then proceeded to dramatically scale back all his community giving, the marketing budget was cut to its lowest level in years, every employee was under much greater scrutiny for discretionary expenses, travel and education was minimized, and personnel was scaled back.

You can't really argue with control of expenses. In his case, he felt his ROI should be higher, to the level of his peers. But here's the unusual facts that he seemed to be missing.

At the time, non-interest expenses (excluding salaries and occupancy) as a % of averages assets under management were at .57%. The average expense level of peer organizations was .56%. This was certainly a little higher, but the organization had made certain conscious spending decisions that were included in this area, such as major community profile (naming rights), and a few very large community contributions, etc. This past investment strategy had dramatically escalated their brand name in the community.

Further under this overall expense focus area was his data processing cost and the organization had just made a significant investment in this, unlike several of his peers. This is not an insignificant difference in weighing and comparing operational choices and their expense impacts.
I looked at his salaries in the same manner, and while his unionized status was unique amongst his peer organizations, and the cost on the frontline alone was known to be approximately 25% higher than those of his non-union peers, the salary percentage was right on the peer level at 0.89%.

It is a pretty simple exercise to see that his organization had really NOT been excessive in discretionary expenses, in fact one might argue that normalizing the comparison by taking those extra chosen contributions would actually put them in a category of being more cost effective than his peers— prior to his initiation of any of his new expense controls. Of course, expenses can always be reduced and when doing so, they are hard to argue; and there are times that they absolutely need to be a priority but every cut has a message and ultimately that can have a cost to culture; and in this case, there was simply no evidence that they were needed to the point of such a cultural risk.

So why would a new leader take this tact?

This is a critical question and must be answered in full context to ensure the organization is looking at real problems, not assumed problems. Again, while the tightening of expenses *and* looking for stronger efficiencies in all areas need to be constantly reviewed and assessed, and I will be fully onside with anyone that plans an effective process to do that within the ranks, it can also be a critical mistake if it affects your culture, while at the same time distracting you and actually causing you to miss the real issues.
It can feel good to push forward and get results such as a better short term bottom line by cutting some costs. But feeling good about something that has short-term quick results at the cost of your cultural consistency or a miss at the real culprits of lesser return, and that has longer-term consequences.
The real culprit for my colleague was not his expense side at all. In fact, a closer look at his margins indicated that he was significantly behind on all fronts to his overall peers and his main

competitor. A further deep dive demonstrated that the company's main competitor was being blamed by his team for ratcheting rates down on the mortgage side and up on the investment side, thus forcing his organization to match rates and drive his margin down. But in actual fact, that competitor had a much higher margin. Simple math again would show that if the margin of his peers and that of his main competitor were matched by his organization (both examples of peer were about the same by the way), he would have increased his ROI by a significant rate, millions in fact.

By overall scale it could not really be just his pricing on individual products that seemed complicit but his Treasury department's decisions on investment and hedging that were clearly the main culprits of his weakened ROI. Sometimes the real problems can be hidden by the distraction of chasing things down a rabbit hole, as the exhilaration of the chase takes hold.

The math is simple in all business, your prospects are controlled by two little factors; margin and volume. There are times that margin need support and times when it becomes a volume issue. Understanding each and the variable factors of how each is determined, will be the difference between success and failure and the difference between long-term success and inevitable failure is how well you've studied these subtleties.

Don't jump to conclusions, and don't rely on the easy answers. Know the problem intimately and soundly before rushing to a solution.

In this leader's case, he rushed to a solution, in my opinion and has already affected a cultural change, whether he is aware of it or not. The messages he is sending and supporting to his employees, his community, his partners within that community, and ultimately to his customers may be permanently impacted. Maybe he can balance both, but my suggestion is he will move his organization back three steps for every cost cutting step he makes forward. He is tasked with selling his FI and if that FI's identity is the cheapskates in the community, that don't contribute (especially on the heels of a previous high profile approach that has now changed), the brand will certainly weaken.

The other key to all business is in understanding and allowing for capital. You cannot run a successful business, no matter how prime the opportunity, or brilliant the idea, or fantastic the culture, if you cannot capitalize your business.

I sit on a couple of Boards for small start-up type businesses and they have dynamic leaders, strong Board members and very bright futures but every caution we make as Board members is to ensure they have allowed and planned for appropriate capital. The business needs tangible fuel to run the engine, once running, opportunity, concept, leadership and ultimately that leaderships build of culture will make it perform but you cannot forget the fuel.

And a great story and set of evidentiary research to back up the conclusions for your story will provide opportunity for that fuel. Lenders and investors ultimately look at your proposal as a story with research or homework that backs up your conclusions, assumptions and assertions.

The process of this story building is critical to capital accumulation and future capital sources but its also a tremendous confirmation to you, as you do the due diligence that this will hold water and be a success.

Even if you are managing a business rather than in a start-up, the Board or Executive team that has entrusted you will want to hear where you plan to go, why you think you can get there, what those ideas are based on, and how you have confirmed (where you can) that the assumptions applied are reasonable. And you do too!

Do your homework, especially the math, and then let the passion move the business. And once you have the logistical stuff in place, never forget:

"Culture eats strategy for breakfast."
-Peter Drucker.

And you choose your culture every day, in every choice you make. You have complete control of your life whether you believe it or not and you can choose many paths through many decisions. It's up to you…

Choose well.

Choices: Your Life is What You Make It   *Kelly McGiffin*

Special Thanks

Choices: Your Life is What You Make It   *Kelly McGiffin*

Choices: Your Life is What You Make It   Kelly McGiffin

I want to thank my family in the close of this book. My wife Denise, has been my partner in this life since I was 20 years old. We've raised three children together (Aaron, Morgan and Robinson) and they've blessed us with four grandchildren (Jackson, Judah, Dechlan and Hana). And we've been doubly blessed in the privilege of raising Jackson fulltime in concert with Morgan.

  Denise and I have now been married for 42 years and together for 44. She has been through every peak and valley with me and never once shown a waiver in her support for me. When you are pushing through life and often times making your own mistakes along the way, having a partner that supports you through every bump along the way and makes you feel you can do whatever you set your mind to, makes it easy to take the necessary hard roads that you need to.

  She has sacrificed her home town, moved away from her parents and siblings, been a rock in raising our kids, and worked her butt off in her own career, right up until her retirement. Denise is an upbeat, outgoing, athletic woman that amazes our friends with both her patience for me and her seemingly endless energy supply. Once on vacation at a resort with two other couples, we were walking to catch a bus into town when we suddenly saw the bus already parked and we were half a block away. Denise said she'd run ahead and hold the bus and as she started to run, the bus started moving. She took off like a bolt and caught that bus and made him wait for the rest of us. As she was heading down at full speed, one of our friends looked at the other and said, "Wow, she's a life saver but I will admit that some days I wish we could just take one battery out of that girl."

    I don't know what I'd have done without that battery or that girl through my life's journey. She hasn't been the woman behind the man, she's my equal, my superior, my motivation and everything we've experienced has been together. I am blessed that the choices we've made in this journey were almost all choices we made as a couple and as equals.

Choices: Your Life is What You Make It   *Kelly McGiffin*

Choices: Your Life is What You Make It   *Kelly McGiffin*